In the Name of God, the All-Merciful, the All-Compassionate

SURRENDERING TO GOD
UNDERSTANDING ISLAM IN THE MODERN AGE

SURRENDERING TO GOD

UNDERSTANDING ISLAM IN THE MODERN AGE

Eren Tatari

TUGHRA
BOOKS

New Jersey

Published by Tughra Books
345 Clifton Ave., Clifton,
NJ, 07011, USA

www.tughrabooks.com

Library of Congress Cataloging-in-Publication Data Available

ISBN: 978-1-59784-270-9

Printed by

Tel : 0212 451 70 70 (pbx)
www.empatimat.com.tr

Contents

Acknowledgements

I am infinitely thankful to God for creating me from nothing, giving the potential to reflect the manifestations of His Divine Attributes (*Asma al-Husna*), and bestowing the ability and the aspiration to write this book. He has placed certain people in my life whose illuminating hearts guided my spiritual journey and led to the completion of this book. I dedicate this book to my dearest friends Karin and Andrea, whose love of God and unending questions about Islam inspired this work.

English translations of the Qur'anic verses are from *The Qur'an with Annotated Interpretation in Modern English* by Ali Ünal (The Light Publishing, New Jersey, 2008).

Please contact me with your comments or questions at etatari@gmail.com.

Foreword

Eren Tatari and I met in college in the years following the terrorist attacks of September 11, 2001. These tragic events had provoked a myriad of emotional responses from the student body, and many individuals were concerned that a rift might develop between Muslim students and students of other faiths. In an effort to promote inter-religious dialogue, several Muslims and Catholics formed a discussion group. We began to meet regularly to teach each other about our respective faiths and share our personal experiences with the God that we all worshipped.

When I was first invited to the faith sharing group, I had no substantive knowledge of Islam and therefore no expectations about what I would learn. However, I was immediately surprised by the many parallels between Catholic and Islamic theology. I was awed that so many Muslims and Christians around the world worship the same God, and that their descriptions of Him are strikingly similar despite certain differences. I was deeply inspired by the love, devotion, and humility displayed by my fellow students as they submitted to God through Islamic practices.

Of all of my acquaintances from the interfaith group, I developed the closest relationship with Eren. I was drawn to her solid intellectual reasoning and her obviously joyful relationship with her Creator. We met frequently to talk over a cup of tea, and as I left, I always had the feeling that God had revealed some important truth to me through our conversation.

In many ways, reading this book is like sitting down to have a cup of tea with Eren. The work is in a category all its own; it is neither an academic survey of Islamic theology nor an attempt to seek converts. Instead, Eren patiently shares precious jewels of wisdom gleaned from the Islamic tradition to readers of all backgrounds. It is my hope that readers will not focus on the theological differences they may find between their own beliefs and Islam, but instead open their hearts to the book's universal message to love and submit to God.

Clare Corado
Indianapolis, August 2010

Part I

Introduction

"When I became a Muslim, I learned how to pray like a Muslim, I learned the Arabic jargon, yet I did not learn how to think and feel like a real Muslim... I thought my paradigm shift happened four years ago when I embraced Islam, but I realized at this retreat that it did not happen yet. I was still thinking with a secular mind. Being Muslim does not mean getting Arabized or learn the do's and don'ts..."

Elijah Reynolds, Indiana University, Bloomington

Unlike Elijah, I was born into a Muslim family in Turkey as the last of four children. My parents sought to raise us with values that were based on Turkish culture, their social class, and occasionally religion. Yet, this concern to instill Islam in their children was often shadowed by more "important" goals such as which schools we attend and how many languages we speak. I remember getting into an argument with my mother over why I was not allowed to date in middle school while my two elder brothers were allowed to date whomever they pleased. The answer I got, which left me utterly frustrated, was that it is acceptable in our society for men to date, but if a girl dates, what would people say. You can imagine how this justification barely held ground for a thirteen year old trained to question. Sure enough, it was not long before I could reason my parents out of any argument pertaining to the cultural norms they wished me to abide by. They finally gave up, and I proved my individuality and the frailty of their assertions. How naïve was I to feel triumph in crashing my parents' good-intentioned efforts to help me stay above water. Given their upbringing and the dire state of our society, they were doing the best they knew.

Unexpectedly though, I began to unearth the truths veiled behind some of these cultural norms years later, in the middle of Pennsylvania. I was attending a liberal arts college, trying to make sense of who I was, as opposed to who *they* were. It is only when you are a fish out of water that you start contemplating who you are and what water really means to you. After years of wandering around to fulfill my inner search for happiness, I finally had an epiphany. No, it did not come to me in a dream—though it would have been much less painful if it had. I had an epiphany in the midst of one of the most painful emotional experiences that a young adult can go through: heartbreak. When my make-believe world all of a sudden shattered, I found myself desperately seeking God. In fact, it was not a purposeful search for God but rather a search for meaning and something to ease the pain of losing my fake bubble of security. I did not realize then that there is no guarantee for any of our plans to actualize. Yet, we often make ourselves believe that they somehow will. When small things do not go as planned, we make minor adjustments to our dreams and move on. It is only when we encounter a huge blow that we get traumatized enough to question the meaning of life. In retrospect, I see that this heartbreak was one of the best things that happened to me in life!

Similarly, another defining event in my life was my elder sister's death at the age of nineteen. Soon after she started college, my sister was diagnosed with cancer and died one year later. I was only twelve. Upon her death, I was convinced that it was impossible to enjoy anything, while knowing I too would die sooner or later. Undoubtedly, because of this traumatizing experience, I began questioning the meaning of life at such an early age. However, it was years later that I was able to pursue these questions and not give in to popular culture that promotes seizing the moment because life is too short. Indeed life is too short. That is why it is also too precious to waste. Hence, we should try to find answers sooner rather than later so that we can truly enjoy, understand, appreciate and cherish life. Despite the immense grief at the loss of a loved one, I am infinitely thankful for this wake-up call.

In my junior year in college, I began reading the translation of the Qur'an. I knew nothing about Islam other than the culturally diluted values ingrained in Turkish society. With the heartache that I was going through, Qur'anic verses spoke to me so strongly and compassionately that the message was hard to resist. It is possible that in such a state, whatever message I came across, I would have held onto its rope, just as a person drowning in a stormy sea. Yet, my story with Islam, or I should rather say, my struggle with Islam, did not end there. It had just begun. However, reading the Qur'an and embarking on a journey of soul searching helped me through those hard times. But to this day, my questioning does not cease. I have learned that this natural (from *fitrah*) questioning is a gift of God to find Him, and in numerous Qur'anic verses, He urges us to question everything.

So why did Islam become so appealing to me at that moment, despite the fact that I was raised in a predominantly Muslim country, by Muslim parents? Perhaps it was precisely, because I was raised with a culturally diluted Islam that was not particularly attractive and convincing to me. I observe now that most aspects of Turkish culture are based in Islamic principles and morals. Yet without sound knowledge of Islam, it was difficult to tell what was from Islam, what was from pre-Islamic Turkish culture, and what was of outside (Western or otherwise) influence. There were only a few people around me who could explain the wisdom behind these values. Yet, we get two conflicting messages from popular culture and from those trying to hold on to religious/cultural values. Popular culture vacuums us with such a strong suction that few parents have any impact on their children. Although God constantly speaks to us and guides us through events, people, and inspiration, negative influences on our freewill are also plenty. God brings a certain constellation of events in our life when we become more receptive to heed His message. As God says in the Qur'an, we need to be ready and receptive for God's message to enter and transform our hearts:

> ...those who were granted the Book before may become certain
> (that Muhammad, who explains everything revealed to him
> without any hesitation in the face of all antagonism and derision,
> is God's Messenger), and those who believe may grow firmer in
> faith; and that both they who were granted the Book before and
> the believers may feel no doubt at all; and those in whose hearts

> there is disease and the unbelievers may say: "What does God
> mean by this description?" (al-Muddathir 74:31)

Finally, in my opinion, the most important reason why the message of the Qur'an got through to me was because God sent certain people into my life who emphasized faith (*iman*) before action (*amal*). For years, they had been studying Said Nursi's *Risale-i Nur Collection* and attending study circles to understand the Qur'anic approach. Nursi is an Islamic scholar who has written a rather unusual exegesis of the Qur'an in the second half of the twentieth century. Traditionally, Qur'anic exegeses take a step-wise approach and explain each verse in order. However, the *Risale* is a thematic exegesis based on the overall message of the Qur'an (the Qur'anic paradigm) and faith (*iman*). And so, I was fascinated with the *Risale* and went "study circle hopping" to understand this complex text. What intrigued me the most about Nursi's approach was its method of building faith from scratch and its emphasis on the process of confirmation through witnessing the inalienable bond between faith (*iman*) and practice (*amal*). Learning about faith became a quest, an intellectual and heart-felt challenge that I was more than willing to undertake. I realized that this was the only way to find inner peace and set my unending qualms with life to rest.

I assume the sheer thrill I get from learning the Qur'anic approach/paradigm is self-evident by now. I have made it a point to take notes during the study circles and have been writing faith-based articles for many years. This book is a compilation of such articles written for various journals, blogs, lectures and sermons. It reflects my understanding of Islamic principles; it is not an authoritative book on Islam. Let's now embark upon this life-altering journey: the process of confirmation (*tasdiq*).

If there is one thing that I hope to share in this book, it is that: a) there is a difference between Muslim with a capital M and *muslim* (submitter) with a lower case m; b) this difference is extremely significant for our spiritual journey. This book is on the process of submission (*islam*) and being a submitter (*muslim*). The following verse, which literally shocked me when I first heard it, refers precisely to this difference (between Muslim and *muslim*):

> (Some of) the dwellers of the desert say: "We believe (amanna)."
> Say (to them): "You have not believed (tu'minu). Rather, (you should) say, 'We have submitted (aslamna) (to the rule of Islam),' for faith (iman) has not yet entered into your hearts. (al-Hujurat 49:14)

Given that this is a scripture that claims to speak to all humanity for eternity, this verse must be speaking to us today. When I think of it in this way, the fine difference that is pointed out is mind-boggling: What is "*aslamna*" and what is "*amanna*"? And what is the difference between them that makes it so crucial for God to correct us?

A Brief Overview of Islam

Islam means submission.
Muslim is the one who submits.
I am a *muslim* while I submit.

B y default, all creation submits to God's will, therefore everything is *muslim* (submitter). For instance, we can witness how a tree submits to God's laws and acts in God's name to fulfill its purpose of creation (i.e. to bear fruits and to manifest God's Attributes). No tree revolts against what is decreed upon it. Trees have no choice but to submit to how God creates them. In the Qur'an, God asks all humanity not to believe blindly, but to witness the truth by using their God-given faculties: their eyes, intellect, and other senses. For instance, God says in the Qur'an:

> But do they, then, never observe the sky above them (to ponder Our Knowledge and Power; and reflect) how We have constructed it and adorned it, and that there are no rifts in it? (Qaf 50:6)

Belief (*iman*) in Islam means certainty, to be absolutely sure through witnessing. Belief is to bear witness that nobody or nothing other than God has the power to create or to sustain anything. It is to witness and affirm that God is the only and ultimate Creator. This is the meaning of the maxim of Islam, "There is no deity but God" (*Lailaha illallah*).

God also asks us to witness this reality within ourselves:

> We will show them Our manifest signs (proofs) in the horizons of the universe and their own selves, until it will become manifest to them that it (the Qur'an) is indeed the truth. Is it

not sufficient (as proof) that your Lord is a witness over all
things (just as He is witnessed to by all things)? (Fussilat
41:53)

So then, how are we a sign to the existence and sovereignty of
God? To comprehend this, we need to reflect more deeply on who
we really are. Are we powerful? Do we sustain ourselves? Do we
own our body? Did we choose our gender, our race, our nose? Let's
do an experiment that might reveal our weakness (*ajz*) and poverty
(*fakr*). When we move our hand, do we really know how it moves?
Do we just want to move it and it moves? Even if we were to master all the specific mechanisms of neural transmission and muscle
movements, we do not put these in action for our limbs to move.
Who then moves it? We often answer this question by citing our
muscles and nerves as responsible for our actions. In reality, this is
not an answer but just a description of the series of anatomical
mechanisms taking place.

The Qur'an confronts us with our reality to provide the answer.
All we have is our partial-freewill (*al-iradah al- juziyyah*) to propel the
movement of our hand. God creates the movement since He is the
All-Powerful and to Him alone belongs all power. This is not to
reject the science of medicine, but rather to say that it is God who
creates the neurons, muscles and the chemical processes. It is to say
that our cells, molecules and atoms do not have the knowledge or
power to carry out their functions.

God reveals in the Qur'an that Islam (submission to the truth
and to God's Will) is the final and complete Divine message pro-
claimed by the last Prophet and that it is a trustworthy and straight
path leading to our Creator. The goal and outcome of submission is
living as if seeing God and doing everything only for His sake. Thus,
there is no separation of religion from daily life, because submission
means realizing God's presence in every second.

Islam consists of the eternal message from the Creator to humanity as outlined in the Qur'an and the teachings and sayings of Proph-

et Muhammad and the other Prophets, peace be upon them all, who lived the Divine message. Belief (*iman*) is to be carried out in our actions (*amal*). Hence, actions not supported by faith and faith not supported by actions do not attain their goal, which is to bring us closer to God. Islam unifies faith, action, and establishes all aspects of practice in this life.

In the Scriptures, God addresses humanity, urging us to do what is good for both this life and the next through our own freewill. God promises inner peace in this life and eternal happiness in the Hereafter, for those who heed His call. The All-Wise Creator, who knows His creation the best, shows the way to truth and good deeds. Since God knows His creation the best, Divine Guidance suits human nature, its tendencies, and capabilities. God's guidance in the Scriptures helps to fulfill our purpose of creation. For example, if we buy a high-tech juicer, we should read the manual carefully so that we will get the best results and not break the machine. If we do not heed the messages of the manual, we would break our juicer, not get any juice, and be upset. Likewise, since God is the owner and Creator of this machine (human soul and body), He knows best how it operates and provides a manual. In this context, God's guidance outlined in the Divine Scriptures is universal, eternal, and not subject to change through time or place.

It is important to realize that God bestowed on us these Guidebooks because of His Compassion for us. A helpful analogy is the syllabus and the textbook provided by a professor. If our professor gives us a clear syllabus and a book explicating the content of the course at the beginning of the semester, it helps us to learn and accomplish what the professor intended for us to achieve in the course. In this same way, since God loves us and has infinite compassion for us, He does not leave us without guidebooks that help us to enjoy and succeed in this life and the next. When we, as created beings, follow our Creator's guidelines, we become blessed with peace in this life, and as a result, will live in the Hereafter for eternity.

Living a life of submission, we benefit from the lawful bounties of this world by concentrating on pleasing God. If we are conscious of God's message and our practices are in line with His Will, we can achieve complete freedom from all attachments but God, worshipping Him alone. We love and respect all created things because of their Creator. Now, let's briefly examine how the Qur'an responds to the following existential questions:

- From where and by whose order did I come to this world?
- What is the argument and evidence to support it?
- Why am I here?
- Where am I going?

According to the Qur'an, the purpose of creation is to know, love and worship God. If we do not know God, we cannot love Him. And if we do not love Him, we cannot worship Him with awe and love. Knowledge of God is experiential. It is not information that we hear and memorize. God makes Himself known to us through His creation. That is, His Revelations and everything in every instance manifests God's Divine Attributes of Perfection (*Asma al-Husna*). In fact, the raison d'être of this creation is to make the Creator known to us. Acknowledging the magnificence of the Creator by observing His creation inspires us to worship and serve Him. Hence, constant worship and servitude is the way to know God in this life. Worship and servitude do not come after we know God, but are in fact the way to get to know Him. This life is a journey where we receive many experiential letters that make God known to us. As we get to know Him more, we love Him more. The more we know and love Him, the more this journey becomes exciting and meaningful.

According to the Qur'anic paradigm, all beings in the universe are letters/signs (*ayah*s). They are written and created to explain the meaning of God through their symbolic meaning. In other words, all beings make known the Attributes of the Creator. With sickness and health, we come to know The Healer. With hunger and food, we come to know The Sustainer. With afflictions, we come to know The

Compassionate. With our wrong doings, we come to know The For-giver. And with our weaknesses, we come to know The All-Powerful. When we look at everything around us from this perspective, life becomes an enjoyable and adventurous quest for The One. Every-thing and every occasion become special letters and gifts from Him whom we are created to know, love and worship. Thus, reason and emotion are God-given tools to observe and reflect on the universe, and to witness the Revelations and His Divine Attributes manifested through His creation.

Science also investigates creation and tries to outline how things happen. The Qur'anic view does not contradict science. In contrast, it perceives all natural sciences in congruence with their Divine pur-pose: as letters revealing the knowledge of God to teach us about our Creator.

On the other hand, materialist philosophy and positivist science looks at things as nominative and attributes power, will and intellect to each thing. As a result of this view, life becomes like a battle of the wolves, and the idea of the "survival of the fittest" is forced upon us. The Qur'an teaches us that nothing save God possesses any power whatsoever:

> If God touches you with affliction, there is none who can
> remove it but He; and if He wills any good for you, then there
> is none who can hold back His bounty. He causes it to reach
> whomever He wills of His servants. He is the All-Forgiving,
> the All-Compassionate. (Yunus 10:107)

Hence the Qur'anic view does not contradict pure science seek-ing to understand the manner and order in which things occur. In contrast, the Qur'an perceives all natural sciences in congruence with their Divine purpose: as letters revealing the knowledge of God to teach us about our Creator. However, the Qur'anic view contradicts the materialist philosophy and positivist science that attributes the qualities of the matter it observes to the things themselves (e.g. the leaf itself is doing the photosynthesis). In many ways, the Qur'an is the expounder of the universe. Furthermore, the universe itself is regarded as the embodiment of the Qur'an by expressing the Qur'anic paradigm in a physical form. Since both are written and created by the same author, there is no contradiction between physical and Qur'anic laws. Thus, when we reflect on the universe from this perspective, everything from a tiny ant to a distant twinkling star helps us to know and love God, and to understand the reality and purpose of the universe and human beings. The proof for Divine existence and unity, Prophets, revelations, existence of angels, and resurrection is logically deduced from observing the universe. Thankfully, these are not abstract facts divorced from life and reality which we have to believe blindly.

It is important to clarify the meaning of worship and prescribed rituals in Islam. Worship does not mean to constantly pray or to be in a mosque or church. To the contrary, most worship in Islam is done while we live our lives. Worship entails being God-conscious in our daily lives. Thus, everything (including eating, sleeping, walking, working, studying, doing sports, and even marital relations) is considered worship if done for God's sake and within the limits He prescribed. For instance, if we eat reflecting on God and enjoying His bounties, growing in thankfulness, and praying to strengthen our bodies to do good deeds, then the act of eating becomes worship. On the contrary, if we eat only out of animalistic need and desire and think that the money we earned secured us the food, then we act in disbelief—that is, we lose the opportunity to know and worship our Creator. This is only one example illustrating that there is no separation of life and religion in the path of submission.

God prescribed certain types of worship to remind us of our Creator and our purpose in life as well as to discipline our egos. For example, Muslims pray in a prescribed form five times a day. Each Prayer takes about five to ten minutes, and they are scattered throughout the day to keep our concentration on God without being swayed by worldly things. By maintaining a God-conscious state, we can transform our daily routine into continuous worship. Thus, for conscious submitters, the five time Daily Prayers are the most joyful moments of the day to restate our thankfulness. It is an opportunity to transcend time and all other boundaries and just concentrate on Him, in our struggle to purify our hearts. Declaring again and again that we worship Him and ask help from Him alone, we find strength to continue our lives in a more meaningful way.

Can We Avoid Our
Existential Questions?

I recall a conversation I had with my best friend in high school. I was deeply troubled with my nineteen year old sister's death and was inquiring about my friend's thoughts on the meaning of life given that we will die eventually. Her answer astonished me so much that I could not find any words to explain the deep pain I had in my soul. She simply said "I am too young to think about it!" This illustrates how skillful we are in self-deception and to shun the reality of our death.

Yet, regardless of our age, gender, culture, religion, or socio-economic status, we all have existential questions that beg answers. Where did I come from? Who am I? Where am I going? On the one hand, we cannot help but ask these questions because it is impossible to shut them off. The urge and need to find answers runs so deep in us that we cannot accept any dogmas. On the other hand, our need to avoid these important questions illustrates our reluctance to dig deeper and face the truth. Ultimately, this search for existential meaning is a search for true happiness or inner peace. Otherwise life simply does not make sense, and we cannot truly enjoy anything.

Because of the way we are created, we seek meaning. We seek meaning in our relationships. We seek meaning in life. We seek meaning in material things. And it is impossible to have inner peace and be in harmony with life and the universe without satisfying this need for meaning. We can describe this as being in congruence with our creation (the way we are created/*fitrah*). We are given various faculties such as heart, spirit, mind, and reason. Without the heart (shutting off our conscience for instance), we become like beasts and commit atrocities. Without reason, we fall into the darkness of ignorance and become zealots. Those who shut off one or more of their faculties cannot fulfill their purpose of creation. Hence, being in congruence with our nature requires us to satisfy all our faculties. Answering our existential questions and finding meaning in our lives satisfies both our heart and our mind.

Our egos develop numerous strategies to ignore our existential questions. Some of the means trying to silence our inner voice are alcohol consumption, being a shopaholic or workaholic, excessive TV or other media consumption, and dedicating one's life to family or socio-political causes to the extent that one becomes consumed in them. Others try to deceive themselves by thinking that we can never find the answers to these questions, hence it is pointless to even try, thinking "We are who we are and that is the end of the story." Yet all these strategies are doomed to fail and torment more and more people into depression and disillusion.

We all want unceasing inner peace. In a way, most of what we do in life is an attempt to attain that inner peace through perhaps attending yoga classes, establishing friendships, participating in religious activities, fulfilling our ambition in our career, etc. And indeed we do find temporary moments of bliss, here and there, but seldom does this happiness last. We strive to buy a new car, but the excitement ceases as soon as we take it home. Then, we turn to something else to make us happy and life goes on like this. Meanwhile, we get tired and depressed of this endless quest for happiness and continuous trend of disappointments. We waste our lives in search of something that we never quite find.

But what is happiness really? Have we ever thought about it thoroughly? What are we looking for? Do we seek the fulfillment of our dreams, passions or needs? Is this the aim of our life, and can this pursuit in itself bring us happiness? Happiness is rather transient. We have randomly dispersed moments of joy, followed by moments of sorrow. This is why it is said that life is all about ups and downs. For instance, think of your many shopping sprees and the subsequent plummeting of your emotions!

Even though we have never experienced the feeling of utmost and continuous happiness, we want to be very happy all the time. This desire in itself is a sign attesting to the existence of such everlasting happiness. Is it therefore possible to attain a state of inner peace? To be able to answer this crucial question, we need to face our existential questions and find out who we are and what can make us really happy. What makes us happy can only be something that is in harmony with our creation (*fitrah*). Therefore, the solution lies in being frank with ourselves, our feelings and thoughts, and acknowledging that we cannot be satisfied with temporary sources of happiness. Inner peace is found in accepting our reality as created beings and acting accordingly.

So, who are we and why are we here? Many of us spend our entire life reading hundreds of books, studying for years to obtain advanced degrees, or working day and night to get ahead in our careers. Yet without posing to ponder upon the existential questions, it is all pointless—for death awaits us in the end. We find ourselves in this mysterious world. We feel strongly connected to endless things. We enjoy a sunny day; we smile and feel happy when seeing a beautiful rose. It seems that nature is somehow related to us, and we have a close relation with all creation. But surprisingly, all these things that we like fade away, die, and do not last. The rose dies, the sun sets, friends depart, and in the end, we know that we will die too. In every instance, something to which we attach ourselves dies or fades away; yet, we still refrain from thinking about the deeper meaning. Since death is so real, we cannot help but ask "where am I going and what is really going on?"

The truth of the matter is that these questions are vital for understanding who we really are. Interestingly enough, for all of us, these existential questions are rather innate. Whether we like it or not, they come to us naturally. But many times, we choose to suppress them, thinking they are too serious and are ruining our happy moments. We mistakenly worry that thinking too much about these existential questions would shatter our dream-like world, which is in fact unable to fulfill our desire for happiness. Only sometimes, when our beloved ones die or when we have tragic accidents, we think we must pursue the answers to our existential questions.

We are like guests in a mysterious house, which is full of things that we admire but cannot quite hold onto. We are brought here for an indefinite amount of time, and we are taken away suddenly. It is therefore only naturally reasonable to wonder and want to know what is going on here. What does this all mean? Why am I here, who brought me here, and where am I being taken to? Unless we pursue these questions for ourselves, instead of shutting them off or relying on cliché answers inherited from our parents or culture, we can never be truly satisfied and happy.

When you wake up in the morning, do you say "Life is beautiful" without a second thought? If not, we have a problem of a dichotomy in our life. What is this life all about? Why do we have to work and go though many hardships? These very thoughts are the keys to open the chains that have taken away our freedom to make sense of our existence. Thanks to the sophisticated toys of this age, we try to silence these questions, hence our humanity. Is it not, as Kant says, our reason that differentiates us from animal beings? And did not Socrates shout from centuries ago that an unquestioned life is not worth living?

Every minute that passes dies, and we cannot retrieve it. We try to cling onto good memories. Memories fade away, and we feel sorrow for not being able to live these moments again. Are these memories not giving us pain? Then, we think about our future. It looks like a dark and unpredictable tunnel. We do not know what will happen to us the next minute, and this affects the very moment we are in. How can I get pleasure at this moment if I know I will die sooner or later? What is money, fame, or passion worth if I am dead? Neither the past nor the present can help us. Does life have to be so? If we want to solve this dilemma, we have to keep questioning and seek the true meaning in life. Truth and permanent inner peace can only be found in God.

Do We Need a Religion?

Religion means different things to different people. God uses the word *din* in the Qur'an to refer to religion. *Din* literally means path. By default, everyone has a path. An atheist's path is atheism. A hippy has his path, a workaholic has her path, etc. So even if we consciously choose not to have a religion, we have one—the path of not having a religion. Given this, the question is why we should consciously choose a path that "claims to be" revealed by God?

God creates us with certain physical needs to survive. For instance, God gave us the feeling of hunger and sleepiness so that we eat and sleep to maintain our metabolism. Likewise, God also creates us to believe and to worship Him. Practicing religion is the food of our souls. He creates us, and He knows best what we need. For instance, when a scientist produces a medicine, he also includes the prospectus explaining how to use it. He knows the best way that we can benefit from that pill and how to avoid any harm. If we decide to take all the pills at once, it will harm us instead of helping. Likewise, God creates us and all the things in this universe. He gives us physical and spiritual foods and explains to us how to benefit from them and which ones to avoid. He teaches us how to pray to Him and how to follow the straight path to reach Him.

History reveals that corrupt political and religious leaders have repeatedly distorted religion and abused it to serve their interests. As a result, some people are prejudiced against organized religion and avoid it at all costs. However, we need to realize that a medicine is intrinsically good, and if used properly, it can cure illness. This fact remains true regardless of those who abuse it and harm themselves. Hence, when sound religious doctrines are distorted by ill-intentioned individuals, this does not annul the validity or value of that religion. When studying any faith system, it is necessary to distinguish the religious principles outlined in the scriptures from its imperfect followers.

As imperfect beings, we can only try to achieve the ultimate goals outlined in the scriptures. For example, in the days of Prophet Muhammad, peace and blessings be upon him, and the several centuries following his life, Islam was implemented justly—resulting in an era of enlightenment and unprecedented improvements in human values, social conduct, arts, and sciences. However, as people became decadent and strayed away from the Qur'an, social conflicts, injustices, and other atrocities emerged. The religion stayed the same, but the followers changed, leading to completely different results.

To know what Islam really is, we must look at the Qur'an to learn why God creates us, what is waiting for us in the Hereafter, and what we are supposed to do with our life. The Qur'an provides clear answers for these issues and together with the example of Prophet Muhammad (*sunnah*), are the only criteria to assess the message. Judging any religion based on those who misuse it is misleading, for all religious doctrines tell people to be humble and just.

Another major reason why some people today refuse to submit to God's guidance is the mentality instilled in us under the guise of humanism: "believe in yourself." We are bombarded by TV, self-help books, and friends to have self confidence: to take control of our own lives, live by our rules, and decide our destiny. We talk about spirituality only when it fits into our other, more important plans. In all the Divine Scriptures, God warns against this ego-trap and advises us to discipline our egos with humility. Just because we are given the limited capacity to reason, we deceive ourselves into thinking that we know better than God. This mentality is a grave mistake that leads us to rebel against God's guidance. For instance, as explained in the Qur'an, God created Adam, peace be upon him, and ordered all the angels and the *jinn*[1] to bow down in front of him. However Satan, who is a *jinn*, "reasoned" that since he was created of fire and Adam was only made of clay, he was superior to Adam. Therefore, he disobeyed God's command and obeyed his own deduction. Is our attitude not very similar to this? We assume that we know better than God. Even though He created this universe and is All-Knowing, we obey our egos and try to justify our disregard for God's guidance.

This is exactly why God sent the Divine Scriptures and the Prophets to guide us. Since God creates us and knows our weaknesses as well as the medicine to cure these weaknesses, He sent the medicine (the scriptures and the Prophets) out of His compassion. God created the ego and offered us the medicine to cure it. But He also gave us the choice (partial-freewill) to take the medicine or not. This is where things get really exciting and challenging.

Our souls were created long before we were sent to this world with a physical form, and in the realm of the souls we made a promise to God. He asked all the souls: "Am I not your Lord?" We all answered: "Yes, you are and we bear witness to this." God has created us in a unique way, different from the angels and animals. We have been given partial-freewill plus faculties such as mind and heart to help us use it correctly. Angels have intelligence but no freewill; they do what they are programmed to do. Animals, on the other hand, act by the way they are created and cannot reason extensively. Yet, we can use our logic to find God and to believe. At the same time, we have partial-freewill to obey or to not obey Him. This is why we are responsible for our actions, and we will be held accountable for our beliefs and deeds. This is the toughest challenge in the universe. The angels worship and are not capable of sinning, thus

---

[1] Prophet Muhammad, peace and blessings be upon him, explained the existence of a species called jinn that are made of fire, are given partial-freewill and other faculties to choose between right and wrong, and will be held accountable in the Hereafter. Conversely, angels are made of pure light (*nur*) and are not accountable since they do not have freewill and perform what they are programmed to do.

they are not going to be held responsible for anything. As for us, we have the noblest and most difficult responsibility among all creatures.

It is important though to remember that God is the Just and Compassionate Judge of the Day of Judgment. He does not hold us accountable for what He has not given us. Hence, everyone will be judged according to their capacity, intelligence and willpower. Since *"There is no compulsion in religion"* (al-Baqarah 2:256), everyone is responsible for their own faith and deeds. Faith is between us and God, and no one can change what is in our heart by force. But what about those people who do not believe in God or worship false idols like their egos? God says in the Qur'an:

> Those who believe (i.e. professing to be Muslims) or those who declare Judaism, or the Christians or the Sabaeans (or those of some other faith)—whoever truly believes in God and the Last Day and does good, righteous deeds, surely their reward is with their Lord, and they will have no fear, nor will they grieve. (al-Baqarah 2:62)

Those who do not believe in God or follow His guidance will be rewarded for their good deeds in this world, but not in the Hereafter. For instance, if an atheist helps out in a soup kitchen, his reward is the inner peace he feels by helping others; yet he will not be rewarded in the afterlife (which he denies) for this act.

Thus, the ultimate goal of religion is to guide us to acknowledge our reality (that we are created beings), to discipline and humble our ego, and to submit to God's Will (by following His guidance) in all aspects of our life. This means affirmation by heart and confirmation by actions. In other words, God has given us intelligence and free-will. It is our duty to seek Him and to lead our lives accordingly.

Affirmation by Mind and Heart, Confirmation by Action

We all have the inner urge to seek the truth and to find answers to our existential questions. Are we sure we are on the right track? Do we have a healthy relationship with our Creator? What is the criterion for being a good person? How can we know the difference between following our conscience and following our evil desires or the whisperings of Satan? Our Creator bestowed us with four sources to get to know Him and to fulfill the purpose of our creation:

1. The book of the universe
2. The Prophets
3. The scriptures
4. Human conscience

Although all four are universal evidence to conceive The Truth = God = Al-Haqq, none is sufficient on its own to achieve the thorough knowledge of God. We are created with multiple faculties with limited capacities; thus we need all four to satisfy our mind, heart, and soul. Additionally, they must all confirm each other. For instance, if what we observe in the universe contradicts what is written in the Qur'an, we need to dig deeper until we discover where we went wrong. Since both are written and created by the same author, either our explanation of creation or the way we interpret the Qur'an must be inaccurate.

Academics and philosophers claim to search for the truth, but it is not clear what they mean by the truth. Likewise, science claims to be objective. A scientist claims that all he is doing is observing the water in the cup and stating this observation: "There is water in the cup" or "The tree grows." Yet, these statements are loaded with value

e water in the cup on its own? Can the tree grow
does not grow: It is made to grow! It is incor-
nething is beautiful. Instead, we should say, it is made
...utiful. It is also inaccurate to say "I love." We are made to love.
Since the ability is not from us, we cannot love. As we reflect on our
reality and the reality of all created beings, we get to know our Creator better. Now let's take a more detailed look at the four sources
through which we get to know our Creator.

1. *The Book of the Universe:* Everything in creation (universe) is
as purposeful and meaningful as a sentence in a book. God says in
the Qur'an, *"He has created the heavens and the earth with truth
(meaningfully, for a definite purpose, and on solid foundations of truth).
Surely in this is a sign for the believers"* (al-Ankabut 29:44). In the
Qur'an, God recurrently calls us to reflect on creation; for everything is created with wisdom. We grow closer to Him by contemplating on the universe.

> Surely, in creation of the heavens and of the earth, and the
> alternation of night and day (with their periods shortening and
> lengthening), and the vessels sailing with profit to people, and
> the water that God sends down from the sky, therewith reviving the earth after its death and dispersing therein all kinds of
> living creatures, and His disposal of the winds, and the clouds
> subservient between the sky and earth- surely there are signs
> (demonstrating that He is the One God deserving worship,
> and the sole Refuge and Helper) for a people who reason and
> understand. (al-Baqarah 2:164)

The book of the universe is a universal source of knowledge
towards knowing God. In this context, universal means that creation
discloses, explains, and makes known all the Divine Attributes of the
Creator. Although sunlight reflects on all pieces of glass and droplets
of water, each reflects light according to its own capacity. And so, a
rose or the sky also reflects God's Attributes according to their capacity. Overall, the universe is a universal source of knowledge, manifesting all of God's Attributes.

2. *The Prophets:* The Prophets are all independent, universal witnesses to the truth because of the mission they were given. Prophet Muhammad, peace and blessings be upon him, was responsible for believing in his own Prophethood. Messengers also have to confirm their belief in God, angels, the sacred texts, Prophets, destiny, and the afterlife. This is important because it emphasizes the fact that the messengers are human beings who have the same responsibilities as the rest of us. At the same time, they are the perfect examples of how we can believe in God and apply His guidance in our life. And because they are human beings, we can never deceive ourselves by thinking "Well, of course they are great, they are angels and have superhuman qualities…" No, they have to deal with their ego and freewill as we do. Additionally, God states that we are not to make any distinction among the Messengers:

> (O Muslims! You) declare: "We have believed in God (without associating any partners with Him), and that which has been sent down to us, and that which was sent down to Abraham, Ishmael, Isaac, Jacob, and the Prophets, and that which was given to Moses and Jesus, and that (knowledge, wisdom and Prophethood) which was given to all other Prophets from their Lord. We make no difference between any of them, and we are Muslims (submitted to Him wholly and exclusively). (al-Baqarah 2:136)

3. *The Scriptures:* Since the creation of Prophet Adam, peace be upon him, God has sent guidebooks through Messengers to make Himself known to humanity. So when we approach the Qur'an, we should always keep in mind that God is talking directly to us. Each verse is meant for us, as if we are having a personal conversation with God. It is important, however, to realize that revelation is not the same as inspiration. Everyone gets some kind of guidance in the form of inspiration, but revelation is the exclusive domain of God's Prophets. Revelation is God speaking to all humanity through a Prophet, through words and meaning. The Qur'an claims to be God's word:

> (O community of the believers!) Do you hope that those peo-
> ple (whose hearts have become more hardened than rocks and
> who have continually shown disloyalty to God) will believe in
> you (and believe in the Prophet Muhammad, and in the Book
> he brought and the Religion he preaches)? (It is surely not
> possible) when there has been a party among them that hear
> the Word of Allah, and then, after they reasoned and judged it
> (to be the Word of God), have tampered with it knowingly.
> (al-Baqarah 2:75)

How are we going to confirm this? Through the other three
sources: observing the signs in the universe, contemplating on the
words and examples of the Messengers, and using our conscience to
verify that the message of the Qur'an confirms the other sources.

4. *Human Conscience:* Our conscience is another source of knowledge to get to know God. Yet this is challenging after the philosophical
trend of humanism, which claims that we do not need the other three
sources, and that our conscience is sufficient to find the righteous life
that fits us. We cannot find God or get to know Him without resort-
ing to all four sources. Each one is necessary to find the truth.

What happens when we do not use all four sources? Following
only human conscience is the path of humanism. Following the universe and human conscience together is the alleged way to the truth
in Eastern traditions, such as Buddhism and Hinduism. If we study
the universe, the lives of the Prophets, and the scriptures without
using our conscience, we cannot come to the correct conclusions. A
good example is academics who study the natural sciences, scriptures,
and the lives of Messengers from a secular perspective, yet still deny
the existence of God.

In the second half of the declaration of faith (*shahadah*), the
believer confirms that "Muhammad is His servant and His Messenger." In this phrase, "Muhammad" represents all the Prophets. It is
essential that half the phrase emphasizes that Muhammad, peace and
blessings be upon him, is His servant. He does not possess supernatu-
ral powers that enabled him to be the perfect servant of God. He was

a human being as we are, yet he took the guidance to heart and submitted his freewill to God's Will perfectly. On the other hand, even if Gandhi was a very good man, he was not God's Messenger. Prophets are fallible, but when they make mistakes, they are corrected by God. For instance, when Prophet Muhammad, peace and blessings be upon him, uttered something that he expected to happen in the future without adding *insha'allah* (God Willing), God corrected him through a Qur'anic verse. This is, of course, a message to all of us regardless of time and space:

> And do not say about anything (you intend), "I will do it tomorrow," without (adding) "If God wills." And remember and mention Him (straight-away) should you forget (to do so when expressing an intention for the future). And say: "I hope that my Lord will guide me to what is nearer to right conduct than this (forgetfulness of mine). (al-Kahf 18:23-24)

Part II: Faith

Affirmation by Mind and Heart

There are six pillars of faith outlined in the Qur'an and expounded by Prophet Muhammad, peace and blessings be upon him:

1. Belief in the Oneness of God
2. Belief in the Messengers of God
3. Belief in the Divine Scriptures
4. Belief in Angels
5. Belief in the Day of Judgment
6. Belief in Destiny

Although they may seem like blunt affirmations, they have much deeper and comprehensive meanings that need to be studied further. For years, I assumed that I believed in these pillars, but when probed further, I realized my lack of clarity. For instance, I had no idea what angels were, what they did, and why believing in them was such a fundamental part of being a Muslim. Likewise, destiny was like a black hole, and I was not willing to get into the subject for fear of offending God! Although this is a righteous concern, how can I profess a belief in destiny if I have no clue what it is? For that matter, if the only thing that comes to my mind is the iconographic depictions of angels with wings, does this constitute belief in angels?

It is essential not to take our faith for granted and assume that memorizing these six lines will suffice. If we spend years to get a college diploma, if we spend hours watching the news and gathering all kinds of unnecessary information on popular culture, we can make the effort to learn about what our Creator says in all the scriptures. To this end, in this section, I will discuss the pillars of faith in greater detail from various perspectives.

1. Belief in the Oneness of God

There is no deity but God; Muhammad is His servant and Messenger

In a sense, "There is no deity but God, Muhammad is His servant and Messenger" is the motto of Islam. The motto's literal meaning, that there are no gods but The One, is straightforward. Yet, this phrase carries many layers of meaning, which requires contemplation in order to decipher and implement it as the guiding principle of our life. Unless, we are ready to renew ourselves, we will continue reconfirming our prejudices and dogmas. Islam came to destroy all idols and the wrong ways of the ancestors (such as our parents or popular culture). Thus, we must deconstruct our pre-learned dogmas and wrong perceptions in order to construct the Qur'anic paradigm. The following Qur'anic verses offer essential insights into understand the meaning behind the affirmation of the oneness of God:

> ... To God belongs the East and the West (and therefore, the whole earth: Wherever you are, you can turn to Him in the Prayer). Then, whatever direction you turn, there is the "Face" of God. God is All-Embracing (with His Mercy), All-Knowing. (al-Baqarah 2:115)

Acknowledging that the existence of everything depends on God's existence is comforting to our hearts. We cannot explain the existence of anything without basing its existence on God. Do we

feel this when we say *"there is no deity but God"*? The verse claims that
"...whatever direction you turn, there is the Face of God..." (al-Baqarah
2:115). Is this really so? We turn one way and see our friend, we
turn the other way and see the fruit trees in the garden. Where is
God? Moreover, we claim to be believers, but then say "this is my
watch, the weather is horrible today, this is what I think." Where is
God in any of this?

> God does not disdain to strike any parable—(that of) some-
> thing like a gnat or something greater or lower than that.
> Those who have already believed know that it is the truth from
> their Lord. As to those whose unbelief has long been estab-
> lished in their hearts, they say, "What does God mean by such
> a parable?" Thereby He leads many astray, and thereby He
> guides many. He thereby leads none astray save the transgres-
> sors. (al-Baqarah 2:26)

This means that even the simplest thing is a parable pointing to
its Creator. Whoever creates the world, creates it to manifest His
Creatorship. Creation, in its entirety, is a sign pointing to The Creator. Everything we encounter is a parable pointing to its Creator.
By reflecting on the creation of things, we can begin to understand
the transcendental world. This is confirming the claim *"...whatever
direction you turn, there is the Face of God..."* (al-Baqarah 2:115). In a
sense, we are living in a parable, and we are a parable. Yet in this
verse, God tells us that the deniers ridicule the parable of a fly-not
comprehending its significance as a parable referring to and representing the truth. He teaches us that this is the deniers' attitude.

The verse *"...Thereby He leads many astray, and thereby He guides
many..."* (al-Baqarah 2:26) does not mean that God leads people
astray by creating a (seemingly ugly) bat or guides by creating a
beautiful peacock. We go astray by our misinterpretation of creation, of a bat, or a peacock. We do not see them as demonstrating
the Attributes of their Creator. Only according to our choices (partial-freewill) does God lead us astray or guide us. In other words,

He creates the results of our choices. For God also says in the Qur'an: *"We have only sent you (O Muhammad) but as an unequalled mercy for all the worlds"* (al-Anbiya 21:107). He lovingly and constantly guides us through the Scriptures and the Prophets, but we sometimes choose to go astray.

"Muhammad is His servant and His Messenger" may also be understood as he was appointed to teach how true the first phrase is: "There is no deity but God." Only through the light brought by the Prophets can human beings encounter the mercy and the wisdom prevalent in every creature. Every creation, from inanimate things to social events, is a means to reflect on its Creator manifesting His Attributes of Perfection (*Asma al-Husna*). For those who do not heed the Prophets, the entire creation is a mass of meaningless matter that happen to exist without any reason. Yet when we look at the creation through the light of the Divine Scriptures, we see how this wrong perception deprives us of compassion.

Tawhid is not Solely Belief

Tawhid is usually translated as "oneness of God." However, its literal meaning is "unifying God." Take note that it is a continuous verb! It is not just a belief but is a state of certainty (the literal meaning of *iman*/belief) that we must strive to achieve continuously. It is a reality we are to live by every day. Belief becomes certainty (*iman*) and a means to witnessing God's oneness (*shahadah*), if and when it is lived in daily life. This is what the Qur'an is about: teaching us how to live *tawhid*. All the Divine Scriptures revealed before the Qur'an also stated that there is one God. Then why was there a need for the revelation of the Qur'an and the 23 years of learning and practicing Islam (submission) by Prophet Muhammad, peace and blessings be upon him, and his Companions?

Most of the Meccan chapters (those revealed in the early years of Qur'anic revelation in Mecca) do not talk about social conduct or the do's and don'ts. They talked about existence, how to perceive creation and life. They sought to shatter the attitude that plagues many of us today: "I believe in one God, but I am very busy with other things." These Meccan verses are about transforming all our actions into worship, acquiring a consciousness of *tawhid*, and living in accordance with that consciousness. They explain what *tawhid* is in different contexts and stages of our life. The Qur'an is not only saying there is one as opposed to two gods. Saying "there is no deity but God" is only the beginning. By saying it, we enroll in a life-long school where we will learn and practice *tawhid*...

"There is no deity but God" has been understood in Islamic tradition as: "There is no Provider but God; there is no Healer but God."

La	*ilaha*	*illa*	*Allah*	
No	deity	but	God	
No	sustainer	but	The Sustainer	*Razzaq*
No	healer	but	The Healer	*Shafi*
No	merciful	but	The Merciful	*Rahman*

It covers all contexts of life. For instance, who brings a baby into life, who takes care of her, and raises her from a clueless being one day to a conscious, functioning adult the next? Is it the mother, society, or the Creator of all? Indeed, observing the creation of a baby in the mother's womb and after birth is one of the most unveiled, clear signs that there is no Rab (Lord, Caretaker) but God. However, in today's world, positivist science that leaves out God, who is "The Cause of All the Causes," is prevalent.

Yet, we need to probe deeper to see if scientific explanations and religion are contradictory. Science claims to explain how a seed grows into a tree and then gives fruit from a mechanical perspective, but it cannot adequately explain how and why. God says in the Qur'an that creation of everything is a sign/*ayah* of God, so we must reflect how it is happening. If we look at how photosynthesis happens, we can write pages of reactions. Scientists claim that the cells are doing all these reactions and get a Nobel Prize for this. If these cells perform photosynthesis on their own, then each of them deserves more than a Nobel Prize! The cells require knowledge and power to be able to carry out photosynthesis. Where did they learn how to photosynthesize? Especially given that the many chemical formulas making up photosynthesis took scientists thousands of years to master. Yet, how are they all doing the same thing, in different locations, like a cell in New Zealand and another one in Norway?

Basically, what we observe is that: Seed + Sun + Soil + Water ≠ Tomato. Each "cause" is also caused by another, which has knowledge and power on every other cause. Hence, we call God, The Cause of All the Causes. In the Qur'an, God teaches us that the cell is being created together with photosynthesis. Cells do not create anything, because they themselves are being made. Cells do not have any power or knowledge, but rather, God is the All-Knowing and All-Powerful who creates the cells, the reactions, and all the processes of photosynthesis.

The greatest falsehood of positivist science is its claim to objectivity. Taking God out of the picture is an interpretation, and interpretation is subjective! In any explanation of the world, there is always an interpretation. The way science presents what is happening renders each of the factors (cells, sun, water, etc.) as a small deity in itself. Our mistake is that we often talk of events as if they happen on their own and don't look at them as signs/*ayah*s. To believe that there is a Creator is the beginning of *tawhid*; only then do we feel the need to learn from the Qur'an and apply it to our daily lives. Even if we come to the conclusion that there is one God, it is only through the Qur'an that we learn who this Creator is.

We cannot overemphasize the importance of *tawhid*, because this is the focus of the Qur'an. Only about 5% of the Qur'an (~ 360 verses) talks about the do's and don'ts (*mu'amalat*). What does the rest discuss then? We see that hundreds of verses talk about water, trees, the heavens and earth as signs/*ayah*s. Whatever the subject of a verse is, the aim is *tawhid*—which requires reflection. Hence, if we claim that our teacher is the Qur'an, then we should follow its guidance and focus on *tawhid*. The Qur'an teaches us the process of unifying God in everything we think and do by asking: Where is the cause? This Qur'anic education of *tawhid* (unifying God) shall continue until we automatically interpret everything as signs manifesting God's Attributes. If we attain this consciousness and see everything as a sign, then practice (praying, fasting, etc.) naturally follows. We would be disciplining our egos through the awe of God, rather than the fear of hell.

For instance, where is *tawhid* in our understanding of death? God does not say in the Qur'an that we will return to Him one day; we are returning to Him continuously. For instance, where is my yesterday, where is my past year? Every moment has returned to Him.

When we die at 80, it is only that moment that is returning to Him. All the past has already died and returned to Him. In a sense, this life and the next are parallel; it is not linear (life followed by afterlife).

In the Qur'an, God emphasizes Prayer (*salat*) as the culmination of worship (*ibadah*). Prophet Muhammad, peace and blessings be upon him, says that the prescribed Prayer is the ascension of the believer. Not everyone; just the believer! So if we live all day as a believer (*mumin*), confirming that everything we encounter is a sign from God, only then will our Prayer be the culmination of that state of mind and heart. The gist of *salat* is *shukr* (thanksgiving), which requires us to see His signs, His grace and blessings everywhere and be filled with the desire to thank Him through Prayer. If and when we are living without *iman* in our lives and experiencing manifestations of God's Attributes, then Prayer will not be very spiritual for us. We may still pray out of fear of hell (which is still better than not praying at all), but we will not seize the full transformative potential of Prayer. To achieve this, we need to go through the *iman* education of the Qur'an and work on transforming our mind and heart.

For instance, the period of Prophet Muhammad, peace and blessings be upon him, and his Companions is referred to as the "Golden Age of Islam." The Companions received Qur'anic education from the Prophet for 23 years. This Qur'anic education was the essence of their value—why and how they became the stars of humanity. Without undergoing this Qur'anic education to train and humble our egos, any talk of politics or economic development of predominantly Muslim countries is empty. The Qur'an directs everyone to find and live the truth. It does not only address certain people who happen to be born in a geographic location and call themselves Muslims. For example, in pre-Islamic Arabia, one characteristic of ignorance (*jahiliyyah*) was to help your friends even if they were wrong. What if those who call themselves Muslim are not right or just? Instead of siding with them solely because they are part of a group we identify with, we should focus on what is *haqq* (truth) and seek to implement that truth into our lives. Talking about politics may be an attractive subject, but we cannot build a house before building the pillars! The Qur'an first established the *arkan* (pillars) through years of Qur'anic *iman* education and then went on to building the social dynamics on these pillars. Likewise, we can see that exhausting all efforts to advance scientific innovation is desirable because it serves humanity in a material sense (such as prolonging life spans through breakthroughs in the medical sciences), yet these innovations make sense only after adequate importance is given to improving humanity's understanding of life. Otherwise, we end up having very prosperous nations with people sunk in depression and frustration, as seen in the "advanced" Scandinavian states—which have the highest suicide rates today. Without Godly principles in our lives, we can only find temporary happiness.

Another example of applying the principle of unifying God in our daily lives has to do with love: love of God and love of people around us. When we hear love of God, it might seem like something imaginary and intangible. From another perspective, we may feel a mandatory need to have a strong love for God. However, love of God is neither imaginary nor intangible. If we take the Qur'anic perspective of knowing God and coming to love Him, our knowledge of Him increases. And we come to that point by getting to know the manifestations of the All-Beautiful Names of God (*Asma al-Husna*) in created things, including other people. Rumi has put it brilliantly:

> We love the created because of the Creator. We come to love
> God through love of people and other created things. Loving
> created beings with the right attitude (because of the Creator)
> makes them more valuable in our eyes. We think of them as
> mirrors reflecting God's attributes, and thus we fear to break
> such mirrors!

Yet, at the same time, loving people because of the Creator prevents us from getting stuck at these mirrors, and enables us to look beyond them to the actual source of light. They are only pointing to the actual source. So if anything were to happen to one of these mirrors, say when a flower or a friend dies, we say that it came from Him and returns to Him. It was a temporary reminder of Eternal Divine Beauty; hence, having learned that the source of its beauty is eternal, we do not despair. Likewise, all the good qualities we see in people (or any other creation) are manifestations of God's Divine Attributes (*Asma al-Husna*). So our love for people is automatically directed to God. If the postman gives us a very valuable gift, knowing that someone else sent it to us, we do not necessarily focus too much on the postman (i.e. flower=postman; flower's beauty=the valuable gift brought by the postman; sender of the valuable gift=God). However this does not mean that we will disrespect or not thank the postman.

So what is the source of hatred then? The ability to hate is also given to us by God. We did not learn to hate on our own. We were taught (programmed if you will) to hate. Everything is given to us, and we decide what we do with it. This is where our partial-freewill comes in, and this is why we need the *tarbiyah* (education, training) of the scriptures.

Thankfulness is directly linked to *tawhid*; whereas *kufr* (disbelief; literally meaning to cover up) is a state of ungratefulness that originates from disbelief. Can we be thankful for anything if we do not acknowledge that it is from God? If we consider the source of achievements as a sole result of our actions, we are thankful to no one but ourselves. In a sense, this is where everything loses meaning. Even if we achieve what we seek, a nonchalant attitude dawns on us. Yet, on the other hand, when something is bestowed upon us, a peaceful thankfulness fills our heart. Even when we are cooking, something completely different and delicious comes out through that process. We are surprised and thankful for this act of creation. Anything else would be *shirk* (associating partners with God). So to all those great cooks out there: Don't forget to give a heartfelt and mindful "Praise is due only to the Creator" each time.

Associating Partners with God (*Shirk*)

> Do they associate partners with Him those who create nothing
> and themselves created. And who have no power to give them
> any help, nor they help themselves? (al-A'raf 7:191–192).

If we were to define *shirk* in the most basic terms, it would trans-
late to a belief in but multiple deities. Even though this is the
most straightforward definition, this concept is much more
nuanced and has the potential to creep into our thinking and language on a daily basis. This is why it is imperative to know what
counts as *shirk*. We must not deceive ourselves in believing that Muslims believe in one God and do not commit *shirk*.

In the time of Prophet Muhammad, peace and blessings be upon
him, people used to say that when the stars came into a certain position it rains, thus attributing power and other Divine Attributes to
the stars. Even though we might think we are Muslims and therefore
do not have this wrong attitude anymore, in most instances, we commit the same mistake. For instance, do we not think and say that rain
results through the evaporation of water and the process of condensa-
tion when cold and hot layers come into contact? If this is a form of
shirk, then, are we not to believe these 'scientific' explanations? So is
it blasphemous to say that fruit comes from a tree and that rain comes
from a cloud? God says in the Qur'an:

> Those who have no knowledge say: "Why does not God speak to
> us, or a manifest sign (miracle) come to us?" So spoke those
> before them, a word like theirs. Their hearts are alike. Yet We
> have made clear the signs (and the Revelations establishing the
> Unity and Sovereignty of God, the Messengership of Muhammad,

and the Divine authorship of the Qur'an) to a people who seek certainty (with open, inquiring minds). (al-Baqarah 2:118)

He addresses everyone, not just Muslims (remember there were no "Muslims" with a capital M). He urges us to go and read in the name of God, to look at the tree and to realize the signs of God's Will in creation of a fruit. The Qur'an is primarily concerned with warning us against associating partners with God, such as thinking that the causes in the universe possess power, intelligence, etc.

> If you invoke them, they do not hear your call; and if they heard, they would not be able to respond to you... (Fatir 35:14)

The first verse ever revealed to Prophet Muhammad, peace and blessings be upon him, summarizes the *iman* education of the Qur'an, *"Read in/with the name of your Lord..."* (al-Alaq 96:1): To read the signs/*ayah*s in the name of God. Qur'anic education enables us to read the signs of God in creation and see the manifestations of His Attributes: the All-Merciful, the All-Knowing, the All-Wise, etc. It is teaching us to read and understand a new language: the language of the signs/*ayah*s in the creation. The language is called *tawhid* (unifying God), and the medium of speech is witnessing (*shahadah*)/contemplating by using all our God-given faculties.

Then, we need to put all our effort into learning how to read in the name of God! How will we interpret the scientific facts? Well, nobody is saying that the fruit falls from heaven. There is the seed, the tree and finally, the fruit. God in the Qur'an is challenging the *shirk* interpretation of creation, which takes God out of the picture. To claim that effects are the work of causes is to associate partners with God. Even attributing the redness of the tomato to its exposure to the sun, without realizing that God is the Cause behind all these apparent causes, this is hidden-*shirk*. God says in the Qur'an:

> Yet some choose to take, apart from God, deities that create nothing but are themselves created, and have no power to avert harm from, or bring benefit to, even themselves (so that they

can give harm or bring benefit to their worshippers), and they have no power over death, nor over life, nor over resurrection. (al-Furqan 25:3)

They cannot create anything, for they themselves are being created. The scientific facts are there, and they are nothing but the signs. We learned to look at things in the *shirk* way, attributing the outcomes to causes and calling this scientific. The Qur'an is teaching us the *tawhid* (unifying God) way of interpreting facts. God is the Creator of both the causes and the outcomes. God creates the seed, the sun, the water, the photosynthesis, the tree, and the fruit. Let's break this down step by step.

We take the existence of God for the purpose of this deconstructive analysis and start with the signs that point to the All-Powerful. Every day we say, "This tree gives delicious apples." The correct understanding is "The tree is being made together with the fruit, for it cannot give the fruit on its own." Why? Because for one apple to come into existence, the entire universe has to exist. Whoever is making the apple must also be making the tree, the rain, the clouds, the sky, the earth, and the whole universe. He must thoroughly know human anatomy, our digestive system, the galaxies, the distance between the sun and the earth, the tilt of the earth, etc. These are all signs, and the interconnection between these causes is also a sign. All signs point us to the Divine Attributes of God. The Qur'an is teaching us to actually read in the name of God, not just to say it. If we want to avoid the hidden *shirk* that creeps into our daily life, we need to be vigilant about distorted attributions and realize that everything is constantly being created by God. Prophet Muhammad, peace and blessings be upon him, was sent as a reminder of mercy for all humankind—to teach this language of *tawhid*.

2. Belief in God's Messengers

This discussion follows our discussion on belief in the Creator of this cosmos. Only after establishing the presence of a creator does it make sense to discuss the Messengers. Thus, we are now taking the existence of a Creator as given.

What comes to our mind when we say "Messengers of God"? Why does God appoint some people to convey His message to human beings? What are the function and the qualities of a Messenger? If we say Messengers are employed, we suggest that God made these selections to remind people of their creation. What is it that we forgot?

> And (remember, O Messenger) when your Lord brought forth from the children of Adam, from their loins, their offspring, and made them bear witness against themselves (asking them): "Am I not your Lord?" They said: "Yes, we do bear witness." (That covenant was taken) lest you should say on the Day of Resurrection, "We were indeed unaware of this (fact that you are our Lord)." (al-A'raf 7:172)

After our spirits were created, God asked us all: "Who is your Lord (*Rab*)?" And we have confirmed that God was our Creator, our Lord. Yet, once we are in this world, we partially forget this reality and struggle to remember our knowledge of God (*marifatullah*) through our life journey.

We have a natural disposition (*fitrah*) to submit to a Creator that has control over everything (which we then call God). We have a natural disposition to submit in general, which we might misuse by submitting to those other than God. For example, this morning we had breakfast. Why did we have breakfast? We were hungry and had to eat. We were created in this way; we get hungry, our stomachs hurt and we need to eat; so by eating, we are submitting to the way we are being created. We also have a natural disposition to submit to our feelings: our stress, our happiness, sadness, etc. We are not like machines; we do not just eat and sleep. We are connected to many things in the universe, and we have the need to express our feelings. We also have a natural disposition to forget[2] and go astray by submitting to things other than God. Thus Messengers are needed to guide us on how to use these feelings.

Messengers also help to answer our existential questions. Every human being asks the basic existential questions: Who am I? Why am I here? Where am I going? We need satisfying answers in order to make sense of our existence and have meaning in our lives. Is there anything nonsensical in creation? We might not like pesky flies or spiders in our house, but still their existence is perfect and meaningful in the big picture for the eco-system. Likewise, our creation is not meaningless. If we do not ask the questions and seek answers, our life does not become meaningless; instead, we do not see its meaning. Just like closing our eyes and not seeing the light does not annul the existence of the sun, our ignorance does not render our life meaningless; rather, it temporarily blinds us. We are the only one devoid of light for that time being.

Our Creator sends us instructors to guide us. If an inventor produced a high tech machine without providing an instructor or a manual, the machine would be meaningless. How the inventor would regard the misuse of his machine is also a point to ponder upon.

From one aspect, human beings potentially have the message in the form of natural disposition and conscience. Yet if someone chooses not to listen to her natural disposition to search for the meaning of life, no Messenger can help. Also, it is very difficult to accept advice and hear criticism from a person who is our equal. Our dignity cannot stand when someone treats us as a child. If someone stops us while we are driving and says we were speeding, we ask if he or she

---

[2]   It is noteworthy that the word human in the Qur'an is *insan*, and is driven from the same root with the word *nisyan*, which means to forget.

is a police officer. If not, we do not regard this person's warning. Yet, our reaction and attitude changes drastically when a higher authority is warning us.

Historically we see two lines of people who claim to bring knowledge to guide people. One is the line of the philosophers who use their own reasoning and observe creation and come up with their own conclusions. The other group is the Messengers, those who receive revelation from the Creator. Messengers are not philosophers. Philosophers learn through empirical experience. They make conclusions as a result of their experiences and observations. Their conclusions may be correct or incorrect. Their deductions are based on their limited subjective experience. Thus, we need sound knowledge from the Maker of creation in order to understand its meaning correctly.

Messengers are not the source of the message. They bring the message from the Creator of human beings, hence the All-Knowing. They bring the message with the emphasis that it comes from my Creator. Thus, we need to approach the message as a personal delivery from our Creator. Because we are created, we need a Messenger to connect with our Maker to explain the meaning of our existence. Whoever made us and put us in this world should not leave us alone without guidance. We live, eat, sleep, and will eventually die. It is all pointless unless the real meaning is uncovered. More importantly, God constantly creates us and constantly sends us messages. We constantly receive *ayah*s from the creation, and when we open the scriptures to read, God is speaking to us right there and then!

So there are two important points about the distinction between God and the Messengers:

1. Our Maker creates, knows, and sustains. He is therefore the Authority, the source of our message.
2. The message is from our Creator, not the Messenger himself, so we should obey the message.

Every Messenger is a human being. God addresses Prophet Muhammad, peace and blessings be upon him, in the Qur'an—referring to him as a mortal man. Why do the Prophets have to be human beings? If the Messenger were an angel, we would not be able to comprehend the message with our level of understanding. The message has to be conveyed at our capacity. Our created capacity is limited and cannot have direct relation with the Unlimited Source of the message. Also, Messengers have the duty of acting as an example to other human beings. If they had divinity we would perhaps have said: "Well, he is divine; I cannot be like him anyways."

Creation carries messages from its Creator as well. However, due to our biases and shortcomings, we can never be sure if our interpretations of creation are correct. A butterfly cannot be a sound point of reference for our guidance, because it can be interpreted as a product or accident of nature. Hence, we need a trustworthy teacher to guide us in interpreting the world around us. Another name for the Qur'an is the Furqan, meaning criterion (separating right from wrong). It means that the guiding criterion must be a trustworthy source, which is revelation from the Creator.

Creation is "revelation in action," which needs to be read with the guidance of the scriptures (revelation in words). A butterfly is created, so it is considered revelation in action.

To summarize, Messengers are like preachers to all humankind— explaining the supreme sign of the universe. They are leaders; they lead and we follow. They can be thought of as luminous trees, whose roots are still alive and whose fruits are fresh and sweet. All Messengers declare that "There is no deity but God." They hold a miraculous message, which solves the mystery of the world, answering our existential questions. With the light they bring, the things we may perceive as evil (sickness, hunger, etc.) become affable with the light of this message. Again with the light of this message, the creatures are seen as reciting God's Names and offering thanks. Without the message/guidance, we cannot make sense of the creation and our existence.

Messengers are worshipful servants of God (*abdullah*) who are also manifestations of God's Attributes. In regard to their Messengership, they are proof of the Truth, and the means to permanent happiness. Messengers did not seek political domination in their societies. They conquered the minds, spirits, hearts, and souls of the people through their message of truth. This great task requires one to be the appointed official of a Great Authority (God).

For example, during the 23 years of his Prophethood, Muhammad, peace and blessings be upon him, was the first person to become a servant of God and submit to the message revealed to him. He sought eternal happiness through all the Divine Attributes of Perfection, which are manifested through the creation. All created beings joined in his Prayer with their natural dispositions, declaring: "Our Sustainer! Let Your Attributes of Perfection manifest on us! We too want eternal happiness!" A flower drawing on water through its roots, an animal seeking food with its instincts, an infant nursing. These are all examples of creation asking to manifest God's Attributes of Perfection. Thus, with its natural disposition, each being strives to manifest the Attributes of God reflected through them. Although the created beings are transient in themselves, what they manifest is eternal.

The Path of God's Messengers (*Sunnah*)

I f religion is communication between human beings and their Creator, why do we need to follow the example of Messengers, who are human beings like us? From one aspect, Messengers are like mail carriers who deliver letters from another source. In the Qur'an, believers are reminded to follow and obey God as well as the Messengers. If we obey the Messengers, we will be obeying God. Human beings do not mind obeying God and imitating Him (manifesting God's Attributes). This concept is expressed in a saying of Prophet Muhammad, peace and blessings be upon him: "Assume the way of God (*Takhallaqu bi akhlaqullah*)."

The defining characteristics of the Prophets are not the clothes they wear or the language they speak. We follow the message they teach and embody in their life. It is highly likely that this issue is framed by Western racial prejudices and the Orientalists. Even though Prophet Jesus and Moses were also from the Arab peninsula, nobody ever claims "why should we follow Jesus' example, since he lived two thousand years ago and in the Middle East?" God says in the Qur'an:

> Say (to them, o Messenger): "If you indeed love God, then follow me, so that God will love you and forgive you your sins." God is All-Forgiving, All-Compassionate. (Al Imran 3:31)

The Qur'anic command is rather general: *"Obey the Messenger"* (an-Nur 24:56). How do we obey the Prophet? Human ego is given to us in order to worship God alone. We feel degraded when we start worshiping creatures. We need to guard this sacred sense, not corrupt or misuse it by deifying such concepts as fame, money or lust. Unfortunately, some people have also deified Prophets by misusing this God-given sacred principle of worshiping God alone.

When we are following Prophet Muhammad's practices, peace and blessings be upon him, we must take the utmost care to not attribute any divinity to the Prophet. When we declare faith, we say "I witness that there is no deity but God, and Muhammad is His servant (*abd*) and Messenger." Servant comes first, because we are fallible and prone to attributing divinity to the Messengers. Hence, we need to continuously reinforce the message revealed to Prophet Muhammad and how he exemplified that message perfectly in his life.

> There has come to you (O people) a Messenger from among yourselves; extremely grievous to him is your suffering, full of concern for you is he, and for the believers full of pity and compassion. Still, if they turn away from you (O Messenger), say: "God is sufficient for me; there is no deity but He. In Him have I put my trust, and He is the Lord of the Supreme Throne (as the absolute Ruler and Sustainer of the universe and all creation, Who maintains and protects it). (at-Tawbah 9:128-129)

So he is one of us, and he is there to protect us from harming ourselves. He is very anxious out of love for the believers. If we are a believer, we will find him most kind and merciful to us, because he is bringing the message/glad-tidings (*bushrah*). If we follow the message, we will not harm ourselves. This verse outlines the main characteristics of Messengers. Jesus, peace be upon him, was the Prophet of his time. Moses, peace be upon him, was the Prophet of his time. So this verse is applicable to all Prophets. The Messengers can be compared to mail carriers, for they are not the source of the message (neither are they philosophers interpreting creation and deducing conclusions on their own). However, we understand from this verse that Messengers do not merely deliver the message. If we suffer, the mail carrier is rarely upset. If you receive from the mail carrier a letter stating you have to pay a certain amount of fines and you panic, the mail carrier surely would not care. But Messengers are not like this; they are anxiously trying to help us.

"…and for the believers full of pity and compassion…" does not mean being kind and merciful to only Muslims. Muslim is the one who submits his or her will to God's will. If we overcome our ego and admit that we are being created, and that we must follow the will of our Creator, then we are *muslims* (submitters). Nursi writes that "The practices of the Messengers are like the ropes descending from the heaven. Whoever holds onto them reaches eternal happiness."[3] God speaks to those who submit to God's guidelines in a different category in the Qur'an, particularly in verses that have to do with practice. However, believers refer to all those who believe in God's existence. We may come and join God's religion, but we cannot appropriate it to ourselves.

Nursi says that "The manifestations of the Most Beautiful Attributes of God are diffused within the practices of the Messengers."[4] When we follow the practices of the Messengers (*sunnah*), we transform all our acts into worship. Following the practices of the Messengers is transformed into recollection of the Divine Presence. In this way, while we follow their practices, our ordinary acts become meritorious acts of worship. For through such ordinary actions, we think of following God's Messenger and conceive them as following God's guidance. From this, our heart turns to the Almighty God, the True Guide and Lawgiver. We gain awareness of the Divine Presence and a sense of worship when realizing the manifestations of God's Attributes in our actions.

One who believes in God will certainly obey Him. And the most acceptable way of obeying Him is illustrated by the beloved actions of the Messengers. The One who makes the universe reflect the innumerable manifestations of His beauty will provide a worshipful state to His Messengers. As servants of our Creator, we will then struggle to make our conduct an example for others to follow the example of the Messengers.

---

[3] Nursi 2002, *Mathnawi-i Nuriye*, Vol. 2, p. 1307.
[4] Nursi 2005, *The Words*, p. 372.

Prophet Muhammad, peace and blessings be upon him, said: "My Sustainer taught me good conduct and how well has He taught me." Following the practices of the Messengers is to assume a conduct within the bounds of the Glorious Maker's Attributes. Man is created with infinite innate love for the Creator of the universe. Since we claim to love God, we will try to act in the manner that will please Him. If I claim to love my spouse yet do everything that I know will displease him, is this love? Love is equivalent with the desire to please the beloved.

The most exalted goal for human beings is to receive Almighty God's love. To do that, we must resemble the ones whom God loves the most, i.e. the Messengers. Aisha is narrated to have said regarding the Prophet: "His character is the Qur'an's." As is the case with all Prophets, Prophet Muhammad, peace and blessings be upon him, is the example of the fine moral qualities described in the Qur'an.

3. Belief in the Scriptures

Why Study the Qur'an?

According to the Qur'an, man knows intuitively that there must be a Creator and he understands what the Creator is not, but in order to know Him, he needs revelation... furthermore, since the Qur'an instructs man to strive to know God when he already knows His existence, it must be referring to another kind of knowledge that exceeds man's acquired knowledge. That is, revelation does not just state the obvious; it teaches what cannot be learned without having recourse to its teachings.[5]

What is religion? What is Islam? And why should anyone study the Qur'an? When asked to define Islam, most Muslims usually begin by listing the pillars of Islam. This is not a sufficient or adequate explanation of Islam. If someone asks me "so who is Lauren really?" and I start describing her height, hair color, occupation, etc. I would be describing the outside, but leaving out the essence of the person.

The question "what is Islam?" could be answered through a secular paradigm (which emphasizes the do's and don'ts without the essentials of the why) or a servanthood/faith/*iman* paradigm. An overwhelming majority of people in the world receive secular education, and therefore have secular mindsets and perspectives on life. Tragically, we do not realize that we view even religion from a secular perspective, emphasizing deeds (*amal*) and treating our rela-

---

[5]   Mermer 2005.

tionship with God as a business transaction of costs (sins) and benefits (rewards). Alternatively, we could answer this question through the faith/servanthood (*ubudiyyah*) paradigm, which emphasizes the real essence of belief.

The servanthood paradigm is based on how we define ourselves. Since I am not creating myself, I am a created being (an *abd*). Thus, there is a Creator. Then, the next question becomes, "What is the relationship between me and my Creator?" The relationship between the following words, derived from the same three-letter root, is crucial:

Arabic term	Common English Translation	Concept
abd	servant	We are continuously being created by God; are dependent on Him for everything, and cannot exist independent of Him.
ubudiyyah	servanthood	Acknowledging that we are *abd*; living our servanthood.
ibadah	worship	Feeling, thinking, acting with the acknowledgement that we are *abd* in every second of our life.

Unfortunately, when we look at all the Abrahamic traditions today, we see the emphasis on the outside (the form or the shell) rather than the inside (the essence) of the message. For example, the current state of Muslims and the predominantly Muslim countries suggests that there is something wrong somewhere. The first few centuries after the advent of Islam, Muslim scientists and scholars lead the world in mathematics and natural sciences. They were the vanguard to western civilization. Now, predominantly Muslim countries are behind in all arts and sciences; their economies are suffering and a mixture of laziness, corruption and moral degeneration has taken over like a disease. When young and progressive Muslims see this situation, they take on a constructive process of self-criticism and point out the need for an Islamic renaissance. The question is: Where did we go wrong? What did we miss, and how did we end up here? Of course the answer is exclusively tied to how much we betrayed the spirit of Islam, and how much we deviated from the real essence of the Qur'anic teachings.

Social revival depends on the spiritual revival of individuals. Our goal should be to live with this faith/servanthood paradigm. It has to be ingrained in our minds, hearts, and characters. All of our reasoning, feelings, and reactions must be shaped by the Qur'anic *iman* education. We have to discipline our ego (*nafs*) and transform our hearts. Religion is a burden if our ego is not transformed. We do the mechanics, but our ego avoids the enjoyment of worship.

The ultimate goal of Islam is to struggle to become the perfect human being (*al-insan al-kamil*). God explains the purpose of our creation in the Qur'an as *"I have not created the jinn and humankind but to (know and) worship Me (exclusively)."* (adh-Dhariyat 51:56). We have been created to know God, to love God, and to obey God. Again, note that the word *ibadah* encompasses an overall state of being, continuously acknowledging that we are created beings that cannot exist independent of God. We may never become the perfect human being, but the goal is to be on the path towards knowing God. Yet, how can we actually know God? We get to know God through His Divine Attributes (*Asma al-Husna*) that are manifested in the creation and explained through the scriptures and the Prophets.

The first pillar of faith in Islam is the *shahadah*, which literally means witnessing. So, what are we to witness? We are to witness that there is one God. But how and where are we to witness, for witnessing entails seeing? We are to witness the manifestation of God's Attributes and God's oneness in the creation. This is significantly different than having blind faith in something we do not see. We witness God's existence and the manifestations of His Attributes in our self, in every aspect of our life, and in the universe by reading the book of signs.[6]

---

6   What does it mean for the Divine Attributes to be reflected in human beings, the universe, and the revelations? Please read the Commentary on "God has created man in His image."

Unfortunately, as secularism and positivism crept in, religion has been reduced to being a Sunday mass or a Friday Prayer. It is even reduced to remembering God five times a day in the prescribed Prayers or other prescribed ways of worship as if we are taking a pill or a crash-course on how to be a good *muslim* (submitter). Yet, if we comprehend the actual meaning of witnessing (*shahadah*), then God and religion does not become one aspect separated from everything else in our life. To the contrary, we strive to live with God consciousness every second of every day. We strive to live as perfect servants (*abd*) of God and fulfill the purpose of our creation.

The person, after learning these truths of *iman* and embarking on the process of inner transformation, has to be different than the person before. If I am not gradually becoming a better person, I am only increasing the amount of factual information in my brain. The criteria of what constitutes a "better" person must also be set out by the Creator and not by the transient trends of society. This information does not become knowledge that shapes my feelings, reactions, attitudes towards hardships in life, my personality, and finally my behavior. If I am still the same person, I have become an observant without a substantial change in my essence. Of course, the transformation is not going to happen overnight. In fact, it is a process of transformations that will continue until our last breadth. The goal is to be on this path. It will take a life time, but the process is a struggle (*jihad*) we have to undertake.

If we define belief (*iman*) as merely saying "I witness there is no deity but God and I witness that Muhammad is his servant and his Messenger," then *iman* cannot be increased. Once you say the *shahadah*, you are done and there is nothing more that can be done on the faith front. Why then did Prophet Muhammad, peace and blessings be upon him, and his Companions pray that they would die with *iman*? They were believers, so why would they not have *iman* when they are dying? Obviously, there has to be another connotation or a nuance that we are missing.

We also confess our hopes to increase our *iman*. Is it increased by reading more Qur'an? Praying more? Fasting more? Eating less? Sleeping less? How exactly can we increase our *iman*? The short answer is, we can increase our belief by internalizing the Qur'an and living as Prophet Muhammad, peace and blessings be upon him—for he was the Qur'an in flesh (the perfect example/student of the Qur'anic education). However, we have to understand what *iman* is in order to increase it.

First of all, *iman* is not a steady thing. It is not a fixed thing but a slippery ground where you can either go up or down. Hence, I have no guarantee that tomorrow I will have the same level of *iman*. Belief needs to be constantly nurtured and increased. Otherwise it will decrease. Imagine a balloon: If you support it with your hand, you can keep it in the air and can even push it higher. The moment you stop exerting some force, it comes down.

Why does it decrease if I believe in God and Islam as the true religion? Well, God creates human beings with a nature of *nisyan*, which means to forget. In fact, the Arabic word for human (*insan*) comes from the same root as *nisyan*. We do not necessarily forget that there is a God, but we do live oblivious to the fact that there is a God. Is it possible to know that there is God and that *islam* (submission) is the truth? Yes, it is. This happens when we are negligent of our reality and believe ourselves to be independent of God.

It is all in the heart. Even if I may follow all the *halal-haram* guidelines outwardly, in my heart, I may still be in disbelief (*kufr*). *Kufr* and *iman* are in the same heart. The literal meaning of *kufr* is to conceal or to cover something up. In this sense, *kufr* is concealing the truth, the truth that God is the Creator of everything. If I should get sick tomorrow and expect a doctor to heal me, I am in a state of *kufr*. Whereas if I am aware that God creates the doctor, his knowledge, the pill, and the healing, I am in a state of *iman*.

A *muslim* must act as a submitter, no matter what. Even if the other person involved in the situation is doing wrong, we have to always be a *muslim*. We cannot respond to wrong with wrong. If we

are a submitter, which means we are undergoing the inner transformation, we cannot act as anything else, other than a *muslim*. Submission
would become our nature/*fitrah*/character, and we would not have any
other choice but to submit.

When Abu Sufyan came to the Prophet Muhammad, peace and
blessing be upon him, some Companions wanted to treat him badly.
Yet the Prophet welcomed him with respect and behaved kindly to
him, hosting him in his own tent. In the Prophet's tent, Abu Sufyan
declared that he became Muslim, but outside, he secretly professed
he was not. If at that time, the followers of Prophet Muhammad,
peace and blessings be upon him, did not treat all unbelievers nice-
ly, would they have been heeding the message of the Qur'an? God
says in the Qur'an:

> God does not forbid you, as regards those who do not make
> war against you on account of your Religion, nor drive you
> away from your homes, to be kindly to them, and act towards
> them with equity. God surely loves the scrupulously equitable.
> (al-Mumtahana 60:8)

On the same token, Prophet Muhammad, peace and blessings be
upon him, teaches us "O servant of God, let your love and hate be
for the sake of God, because no one can attain to the *wilayah* (guard-
ianship) of God without that, and no one shall find the taste of faith
without that, though his Prayers and fast be great in number."[7] This
saying has a gist to it that makes the entire meaning different. You
love the *mumin* characteristics, and you hate the *kafir* characteristics.
A non-Muslim may have *muslim* characteristics, and you love the person and the good characteristics; a Muslim may have *kafir* characteristics, and you dislike those characteristics.

Likewise, Prophet Muhammad, peace and blessings be upon him,
said "Help your brother, whether he is an oppressor or he is an
oppressed one." People asked, "O Allah's Apostle! It is all right to

---

[7] Majlisi 1983, Vol. 27, p. 54.

help him if he is oppressed, but how should we help him if he is an oppressor?" The Prophet said, "By preventing him from oppressing others."[8] When he is a *zalim* (oppressor) you are beside him to help him to correct himself, not to defend his *zulm* (oppression)!

---

[8] *Sahih al-Bukhari*, Volume 3, Book 43, Number 624.

How to Approach the Qur'an

When we are studying the verses of the Qur'an, we must keep in mind that while the author of the Qur'an is God, He is speaking directly to us to teach something. When we approach the message, we must be aware that each and every verse is addressed to us by our Creator. Since we know that God is speaking to us to teach us the purpose of our creation, we must try to see how each verse is educating us about our purpose.

For instance, God says in the Qur'an, *"We have not created the heavens and the earth and all that is between them in vain..."* (Sad 38:27). We need to study the creation in order to confirm this claim. When we observe creation, we realize that everything is created (and is being created every instance) to make us know who our Creator is and the purpose of our creation. Thus, we are surrounded by purposeful creation and infinite letters bringing us messages from our Creator. When we study the creation, we observe that nothing comes into existence by chance. Created beings demonstrate that their Creator can only be the Absolute One through the various qualities they have been given.

Our understanding of each verse must be the result of a conscious effort to comprehend God's speech sent to guide us. In the same way, even if a verse may be seemingly simple, when we bear in mind that it is God who is talking, then our expectations and attitude towards it changes. The same is true for God's revelation in words (scriptures) and God's revelation in action (the creation).

For example, let's look at a fig. Do we realize that a single fig has to be created by the One who has absolute power? Unbelievers would take the fig lightly and thus not get its real profound meaning. This particular attitude of unbelievers is deliberate. Since unbelievers do not want to submit to a higher being, they do not accept that created beings have an owner/maker. With this attitude, a fig becomes only a means to nourish living beings. This is equivalent to saying it is created in vain. The Creator of the fig did not create it only to feed us. Its ultimate purpose of creation is to bring news from its Creator and make the Creator known to us.

For instance, if God suggests keeping our houses clean, this suggestion should not be taken lightly at face value, thinking that the only reason is, say, to be healthy. We must approach this suggestion in such a way as to help us build and secure our belief. When we are reading each verse, we have to be mindful of the ultimate aim of the Qur'an, and try to understand each sentence in light of the bigger picture. In a sense, every verse must take us to the transcendental world. Interpretations of Qur'anic verses that lack this attitude have shortcomings and are bound to be misleading.

Before reading the "Speech of God," we need to define what "Speech of God" really means. God speaks in two ways: a) with words (scriptures) and b) with action (creation). God says in the Qur'an:

> They will ask their skins, "Why have you borne witness against us?" They will answer: "God who makes everything speak has made us speak." It is He Who has created you in the first instance, and to Him you are being brought back. (Fussilat 41:21)

These two kinds of speech support each other. God's speech is not historical, it is universal; it addresses all humanity, at all times, and in all situations. When we read God's speech we need to bear in mind the following principles:

1. Who is speaking? The Creator of the universe
2. To whom is He speaking? All humanity
3. Why is He speaking? To answer basic existential questions
4. In which capacity is He speaking? As a merciful God

The general principles of exegesis are:

1. Reading the Scripture to check if it is really God's word

2. Reading the Scripture as a potential elucidator of the meaning of life

3. Abstaining from drawing hasty conclusions; we need to interpret every single verse within the context of the above four principles

4. The stories of the lives of the Prophets and their miracles need to be interpreted in a way that would not contradict the universality of the Scripture

5. Information about the Hereafter is to be interpreted in order to organize our lives here in this world

When studied in light of the above principles, four overarching themes emerge from the Qur'an:

1. The Oneness of God
2. Existence of the Hereafter
3. Messengership
4. Justice and worship

What is the nature of the Qur'an or in general all scriptures? And how should our attitude be towards them? What are the particularities of a text for it to be called scripture? Scripture means the holy or sacred text; God's word as revelation (not inspiration). Prophets received revelation, as well as inspiration. For the Prophets, revelation is when the meaning and the words are from God, whereas inspiration is when the meaning is from God, but the words are not.

So there is the Qur'an, *hadith qudsi*, and *hadith*. The Qur'an is the word of God, brought to the Prophet through Angel Gabriel, and no one has the right to change the words. *Hadith qudsi* is a saying of God, narrated by His Messenger but not included in the Qur'an. The teacher for us in the Qur'an is God. In the latter two, the teacher is the Prophet, but he is not the source of the wisdom or the message. During Prophet Muhammad's time, it was forbidden to write down *hadith qudsi* and *hadith* in order to avoid potential mix-up with the Qur'an. Hence, only the Qur'anic verses were written down during his lifetime.

When we are reading a *hadith,* we need to know the historical event related to it. An example can be reading a saying of the noble Prophet from the Meccan period. If we do not know the verses of the Qur'an revealed prior to this event, we cannot interpret this saying properly. So the Prophet might have acted at this event according to the traditions of the society, since certain verses of the Qur'an were not revealed yet at that time. Prophet Muhammad's sayings as such do not establish the religion. He is not the founder of religion. We can find a Christian, Jewish or Meccan tradition at that event, because Prophet Muhammad, peace and blessings be upon him, applied the common tradition of the place.

Tadrij, which refers to gradual development, implementation, establishment of religion, is a principle of Islam. There is a human tendency to elevate leaders, but we should not exaggerate. Prophet Muhammad, peace and blessings be upon him, was honest to his nature, followed the monotheistic (*hanef*) tradition of Prophet Abraham, and did not participate in any polytheism. As a man, he was honest, and did not do anything deliberately wrong. Yet still, he was not the founder of the religion. However pure his personality is, he was not the establisher of the religion; he was an ideal student, chosen to present God's religion Prophet Muhammad, peace and blessings be upon him, taught his community what God taught him. So, Islam is not Muhammadanism, but the religion of God.

All of the misunderstandings and quarrels among the Muslim community arise from the avoidance of gradual establishment (*tadrej*). Studying the Qur'an and the *hadith* requires scholarship, expertise in history, and well-versed knowledge. The most developed science in Islam is *hadith,* followed by the interpretation of the Qur'an.

The Nature of Divine Scriptures

1. *Descent from God to human beings:* When we read the Qur'an, we must not forget that the word of God is expressed for our understanding. It is coming from the Absolute, Infinite, Unlimited One. Yet, we understand within our capacity, because the One understands who will read it. However, I am mistaken to believe the Qu'ran, since it is simplified to my level, is easy to understand. For instance, if Einstein comes to an elementary school and speaks to first graders, he will try to simplify his teachings for their level. Likewise, the Qur'an is the Absolute One's teachings explained at our level. When people write commentaries on the Qur'an, it is their interpretation/understanding: We are swimming in an ocean, yet all of us have our way of swimming. That is why in principle, if two Islamic scholars contradict on one subject, their opinions are respected and still rewarded for their effort to understand God's words.

We must be aware that we are swimming in the ocean; we are only swimming in our path, and we cannot swim everywhere in the ocean at once. We understand the Qur'an as much as our capacity allows us. The Qur'an is published with no name on it, but when there is a translation or commentary, one can see the scholar's name on it. Most of the commentaries are subjective interpretations. Even if it is written by the best scholar, it is still his or her translation and commentary, not the original. Hence, translations of the Qur'an are not called the Qur'an!

2. *Purpose in sending the revelations*: What is the purpose of God speaking to us through the scriptures?

a) To disclose Himself: to make Himself known to us and teach human beings who their Creator is.

b) To answer our existential questions and help us interpret the creation: We cannot find the answers on our own, but if someone explains to us, we are able to use our reason and other faculties to make sense of it.

c) To help us get out of our own paradigm (or bias): We need another source, an all-encompassing conscious to guide us with an unlimited knowledge and teach us how to interact with the things around us.

3. *Book of education:* Given these purposes, the Qur'an is an educational text; it is intellectual and can transform us. Sometimes, we read the Qur'an not as an educational text that will transform our inner being, but just to carry out the do's and don'ts without reflecting on them. In a way, this attitude is out of reverence for the Qur'an: we take a verse from the Qur'an and say "since this verse says so, it must be so." This is not reading the scripture to learn something from it or to be transformed by it. Reading it as a book of prayer is fine, but it must also be read as an educational text. We should not read the scripture to condition ourselves, to brainwash ourselves. We are told to memorize and recite the national anthem to fortify our already existing prejudices, to condition ourselves. Is it wise to read the scripture like this? We have to read the Qur'an, as if we are listening to our teacher, to learn from it, not to imitate it. We tell ourselves we have to "read in the name of our Lord who created us" but what if we do not know how to do this?

To actually benefit from the Qur'an, we must ask ourselves: Is it really true? Is it possible to read in the name of our Creator? What does it really mean? We need to educate ourselves through its teachings. We will be drawn out of some ignorance. If we are not familiar with this approach, we exclaim, "God says so in this verse so it must be so." But the real question is: What did you understand from it and how did it transform you? From which state to which state were you transformed? When we recite the verse, we must not speak on behalf of God. After we complete our education in nursing school, we go to a hospital and practice, because we must further our education. If someone is my nurse and she takes care of me perfectly, I ask: Where did you learn this? They tell the name of the school. Likewise, we must learn from and be transformed by the Qur'an, and practice what we learn, so when someone asks how and where did you learn this from, we refer them to the Qur'an.

Sometimes people just "shoot" a verse from the Qur'an to defend a point they are making. Since they are reciting the Qur'an, they feel as if the argument is over because you cannot "argue" with God's word. If we cite verses from the Qur'an, without being transformed by them or give evidence to prove the truth of the Qur'an, this is a literalist attitude. Just relating a verse from the Qur'an and saying "I am not saying anything, God is saying it," is not neutral. You put your interpretation onto it. In a particular context, topic, someone relates a verse, but it is our interpretation that God is meaning this in this context. You, narrating the verse at that moment is an interpretation. When a doctor performs a medical procedure, she is practicing what she learned in medical school. In reality, she may be adding her own take to how the procedure must be done.

There was an argument between two communities during the time of Ali's leadership. One side's position was along the lines of: "Let's make the Qur'an a witness to our argument. Let the Qur'an decide about who is right. Let the Qur'an be the judge." Ali, as a very wise man brought up in Prophet Muhammad's household, brought the *mushaf*, the book containing the Qur'an. He explained that this book does not speak for itself, it stays there, you make it speak. This is in fact the first hermeneutic approach. When we introduce a verse into an argument, we deliver it from our realm of understanding. By locating the verse into our paradigm, we fall into a literalist attitude. It is a crucial but extremely fine point that is often overlooked. This literalist approach, no matter which religion it is framed as, is wrong and deceptive.

Another example is the war between Ali's supporters and Muawiya's supporters. Towards the end of the war, when Muawiya's supporters were about to be defeated, he ordered his soldiers to attach pages from the Qur'an, knowing that Ali's supporters were extremely respectful to the Qur'an and that they would not fight. Indeed, Ali's supporters ceased fighting. As a result of this incident, a well-known phrase came about: "You never put the Qur'an to your spear!" meaning that you do not use the Qur'an to support your point. In other words: "Do not hide yourself behind the Qur'an, and read the verses to justify your own paradigm, ideas. But put the Qur'an behind you if you are a brave man, and come up as yourself to defend yourself. Say this is my understanding of the verse, if you do not like it, it is because of me. Yet the literalists say if you criticize what I say, it is what God says, so you are a heretic. If the nurse does a wrong injection, and paralyzes the patient, and says I graduated from such university... Do not blame the educator, blame yourself. Accept that your interpretation is wrong. Say I have not got good education, I was not a good student, but that university teaches very well."

So when we read the Qur'an, we must be humble and admit that this is our understanding. If someone disputes our interpretation, we can say: "Maybe, it is possible that my interpretation is wrong. Let's go back to the source and try to get educated by it. Let's study together, admitting that we are both students trying to understand the text/teacher." But the literalist says, "I am not saying anything; God says this in the Qur'an. Speaking on behalf of the Qur'an, and if you oppose me, you are a heretic, an infidel." Our personal approach and ideas should not be equated with the original text. We cannot narrate the text to justify our argumentation and claim that this is the ultimate meaning of the verse.

4. *Qur'an needs to be confirmed by the reader:* When we read the scripture, we must always keep in mind that we are its students and it is our teacher. The student listens to his teacher, hear something that he does not know already and needs to learn. Our goal in the classroom, while God is speaking to us, is not to be a parrot, we are

expected to understand and confirm. When the teacher says 3x3=9, some students just repeat and memorize it while others process it in their minds. These students are not judging the teacher, but they need to confirm it for themselves. The confirmation comes a few minutes later. One of the pillars of belief in Islam is to believe in the Qur'an as the word of God: This means to confirm (*tasdiq*) it.

Education (*Tarbiyah*) of the Qur'an

Islamic scholars unanimously agree that the primary message of the Qur'an is *tawhid*. *Tawhid* is an Arabic word that is commonly translated as Oneness of God. Yet, the closest translation of the grammatical form of *tawhid* is "unifying God." In other words, *tawhid* means continuously affirming or confirming that God is One. This mission is also summed up in the declaration of faith *Lailaha illallah* (there is no deity but God). At first it seems like a simple message that there is only one God as opposed to two or three. But is it really that simple? If it was that simple, what were the Companions of Prophet Muhammad, peace and blessings be upon him, struggling to understand for 23 years (the duration of Qur'anic revelations and his Prophethood), sitting beside the Prophet to be educated (*tarbiyah*) by the Qur'an?

Indeed, *tawhid* is at the heart of our relation with our Creator. The truth is simple, thus the statement is simple. Yet, surrendering one's self to this truth is not an easy task that can be accomplished overnight. The following verse may be referring to this fact:

> (Some of) the dwellers of the desert say: "We believe(amanna)."
> Say (to them): "You have not believed (yuminu). Rather, (you should) say, 'We have submitted (eslamna) (to the rule of Islam),' for faith (iman) has not yet entered into your hearts."
> (al-Hujurat 49:14)

Even though the Companions changed their intentions fast and decided to surrender to God's Will, it took them 23 years of education to transform their paradigms and completely surrender; and they were still praying that they would die as *mumins* (believers)!

An overwhelming majority of people today do not claim that there are two or three gods. Yet, one of the major problems of human beings is assigning Divine Attributes to causes. If we see an egg, and assuming that we have never seen a chick coming out of an egg, could we ever imagine that out of this solid, lifeless thing, a creature will pop out? There is seemingly no relation whatsoever between these two beings, a chicken and an egg. So causes are not even apparently effective in producing the outcomes, i.e. the effects. Yet, how is it that we fall into the trap of thinking that the egg "produces" the chicken? God creates everything in the same manner with the same order: For example, He always creates chickens from eggs, never from acorns...[9] So when we observe the same sequence of occurrences continuously, we come to forget the Judge (*Hakim*) and the Creator, thus attributing the Creatorship to the egg.

What are causes then? If God is indeed the All-Powerful and the All-Knowing, can He not create the tomato directly, without the causes? Yes, He could have. But it is part of the big picture/the Divine plan to create the causes and the effects, and to make the causes a "veil" to His Divine Attributes. Let us think of the common message of the scriptures: All of them are reminding us that we have a Creator, and they expound on Divine Attributes of our Creator, in a sense, introducing Him to us. God teaches us in the Qur'an over and over again to ponder upon the signs (*ayah*s) in the creation of things in the universe, and then in ourselves. In a sense, this is our life-long struggle (purpose of our creation) to see, think, feel, and act in the name of the Creator: Not to attribute the qualities of things to themselves; not to act in our name, appropriating our qualities, thinking "I am intelligent, I love, I do, etc."

[9] What we call *mu'jiza* (miracle, literal translation is something that makes you [feel] helpless; makes you realize that you are helpless) is God creating something out of the "normal" order that He always does. For instance, He always creates babies from an egg and a sperm. Jesus' birth to Virgin Mary is a miracle. It is in fact no more or no less "difficult" to create a baby without a sperm than it is to create one from an egg and a sperm. Both require infinite power and knowledge, and the One who possess infinite power and knowledge can do both.

In this struggle, causes play an important role in helping us understand that there is One God. We observe the egg and the chicken, the atoms, and everything else to confirm this truth. We realize that an egg cannot in itself produce a chicken in a million years. We confirm that none of these things own any of the qualities they manifest. After we confirm that even the things that seem to be the most intelligent and superb cannot do a single thing on their own, we turn to ourselves and acknowledge that nothing in us is from ourselves. These processes are steps of submission that lead to certainty in belief in God's existence and oneness.

Let's discuss another example. Each of us is a sign pointing to the Divine Attributes of the Creator. For instance, if I act mercifully, I am only choosing with my partial-freewill to act as a mirror to the mercy of the Most-Merciful God. Also, I am created with an intrinsic quality to love what is beautiful. A flower is a sign pointing to the Divine Attributes of the Creator as well. It has been created beautifully by the Most-Beautiful One; it has been fashioned and designed in the most perfect manner by the Fashioner and the Designer. Moreover, me loving the flower (the relation between me and the flower) constitutes another sign out of these two seemingly unrelated signs. When one ponders upon my reaction to the flower (feeling of love), there is absolutely no way to explain this feeling by materialist philosophy. Why would a creature, made up of flesh, blood and bones (just as a chicken is) suddenly have this feeling upon seeing a flower (whereas a chicken would eat the flower rather than appreciate and love its beauty)?

I just "claimed" that our feelings are also given by God. The discipline of medicine explains feelings through chemical reactions, which are only the causes created by God that cannot create the effects by themselves. The other alternative would be us creating them somehow, or them being created by themselves, or by chemical reactions. All the alternatives connote infinite, Divine powers to causes and hence do not make sense.

Yet, one may ask: If God is creating all the feelings in us, what is the point of anger or jealousy, or for that matter any other feelings that we might perceive to be undesirable? The essential point is this: Indeed these feelings are created and given to us by God, but these feelings, say anger, is not given so we say "I am an angry person, what can I do?" We observe purpose and wisdom in the creation of everything in the universe, thus we confirm that the Creator is the Most-Wise and does not create anything in vain. Hence, we conclude that there must be a wise purpose behind the creation of anger as well. Let's say that we get angry at something. Since we have partial-freewill, are we going to carry on with this anger or are we going to control it? This is the struggle for self-discipline, hence training our ego/*nafs* to accept the reality as it is and not to have false claims of ownership over our intelligence, feelings, existence, etc. This discipline culminates in the fulfillment of our humanity.

The same is true for love. No feeling, be it anger or love, is absolutely good or absolutely bad. It is how we use it that renders it good or bad in different instances. Just as a knife may be used to murder someone, it may help save a life when used appropriately by a surgeon. Thus, we must try to use these feelings, which are "tools", with our partial-freewill to better ourselves, and understand that they are gifts from our Creator given to us for a wise purpose. For instance, anger is meant to be used against injustice or oppression.

How does this all tie back to *tawhid* and the education of the Qur'an? God teaches us in the Qur'an how to look at the signs to increase our knowledge of Him (*marifatullah*). Yet, the purpose of this knowledge is not just to increase our 'information' about Him. This knowledge is to transform us, to educate us in the way of *tawhid*, which is the only way to live peacefully without contradicting ourselves because *tawhid* is accepting the reality as it is. We are to confirm the Unity of God constantly by observing the outward and inward signs. And as we confirm His Divine Unity, we are to submit and surrender to the truth with all our being: our feelings, thoughts, and actions.

4. Belief in the Angels

One of the pillars of faith in Islam is the belief in the existence of angels. But what exactly are they? Angels are created from pure light (*nur*), and they do not have freewill. They perform what they are programmed to do. Angels are nothing but the "carriers" or "transformers" of God's will in the form of beings as we observe here in the universe. Although, there are countless angels performing different duties, we generally know of the four angels and their duties, whose names are mentioned in the Qur'an:

1. The Archangel Jibra'il (Gabriel): angel of revelation, bringing revelation from the Heavens to the Prophets.
2. Mikail (Michael): associated with natural occurrences like rain and thunder, among other duties.
3. Azrail (the Angel of Death): in charge of taking people's souls upon death.
4. Israfil (Raphael): within charge of blowing the trumpet at the end of time.

Colin Turner summarizes Nursi's explanation of angels in his book *Islam: The Basics* (which I highly recommend) as follows:

In accordance with the principle of continuous creation... things which are created cannot themselves create: power belongs only to One. Similarly, knowledge—and with it, consciousness—cannot be attributed to inanimate creation in any meaningful sense of the word. And that which lacks power and knowledge cannot be said to have any discernible sense of purpose. But if we dismiss inanimate particles as unconscious, and their functions as purposeless, how do we account for the myriad wondrous new shapes and forms they bring into being? It would appear that only by bringing 'angels' into the equation can we begin to make sense of this dichotomy.

For angels are 'bearers' of the Divine 'commands'. According to the Koran, when God decrees that a thing come into existence, all He has to do is say 'Be!' and that thing appears. The angels are, in one sense, the 'mirrors' which are held up to the Divine Essence so that the attributes of God may 'shine' into them directly. Man, who cannot perceive God directly, knows Him only through the reflection of the names that he views in the 'mirror' provided by the angels. The angels, then, act as the interface between God and man.

Angels possess consciousness but not free will: their obedience is unwavering, but it is never blind. The apparent consciousness of an otherwise seemingly blind, inanimate being is actually the consciousness of the angels, who 'bear' the creational commands which make up that being's external existence.

Facing God directly, the angel, equipped with the ability to reflect one of more of the Creator's 'names', accepts God's command and proceeds to 'bear' it. They carry it from the unseen realm to display it in the manifest realm, or the realm where the names of God are given a sort of material existence in the form of created beings.

The existence of angels helps to explain why matter behaves with such apparent purposefulness while at the same time exhibiting absolute ignorance and dependence. Yet there is more to Koranic angelology than merely serving to explain why material causes do not actually create anything. For the reflection of God's names onto the 'angels' brings about nothing less than the material world of which we are part. They are like so many prisms which catch the white light of God and refract it into the myriad colors of material existence, so that humankind may come to know and comprehend His true Source. Angels are there, not because God needs them, but because we need them. (Turner 2005, 82–83).

5. Belief in the Day of Judgment and Afterlife

Although we all know that we will die (tomorrow or in 60 years), most of us go through something called the mid-life crisis. We start to realize that life is coming to an end and that this world is not our eternal abode. An Arabic saying goes: "Whatever is in the future, is indeed very near." As long as it is on the way, it will come. For those of us who are still fairly young, 10–20 years later our own mid-life crisis will come for sure. The countdown begun the day we were born. So how important is it for us to believe in the afterlife? Without believing in the afterlife, this life becomes like hell or like living a lie.

As we get older, we tend to seek solitude in loneliness. We realize that no one is a real friend. Not because they are vicious but because they are dying and leaving us, and we are to leave them, too. We cannot hold on to them even if we wanted to. They cannot satisfy our needs. If I am dying, even if my father wants to save me, he simply cannot. The ones we were once connected to and loved have already died. I am not only referring to other people: My childhood is gone; everything we were once attached to is gone, including our toys, money, career, prestige, etc. The pain of separation is in every moment of our lives since we are constantly experiencing it. Not only is the moment of death separation from this world but as far as yesterday's life is concerned, I have already experienced a separation.

To recognize and ponder upon this continuous and inescapable separation is important. How we tend to forget about the reality of life by ignoring the inevitability of separation is remarkable. Yesterday is gone, and there is no way to retrieve it. However, we are constantly told by pop-culture not to think about yesterday in order to avoid the sorrow, and to think about the bright future and make happy plans, etc. We always have a new plan: Enjoy your life, get a career, walk up the steps of life, and enjoy your retirement, etc. What comes then? Death for sure! Yet we do not want to talk about it. Every moment we are being separated from the last moment; this is supposed to remind us that we are temporary beings in this life. We are actually experiencing death in every moment.

Upon the death of our loved ones, we do not cry only because of loss. Yes, it is hard to bear that they are gone. The real sorrow though is due to the reminder that I will die as well. It is a reality of the soul that it does not want to experience death—if death is understood as the end of life. The unbearable feeling when someone dies serves a purpose since it makes us understand that we are not created for a limited life. My rejection of a non-eternal life is proof that there is eternal existence. We learn all we know from experience. Even our imagination is based on things we experienced. Nothing we have seen is eternal. So where did we learn something called eternity? Where did we get the feeling of yearning for eternity? Who taught us this feeling?

When we think of eternity, we associate all the beautiful things we see in this world with it. One of God's Divine Attributes is the Eternally Beautiful One (Al-Jamel). Everything in this universe comes from the source that is Eternally Beautiful. This yearning for eternity is evidence of afterlife. Hence, when we read the scripture talking about afterlife, we relate to it immediately. It confirms our feelings. This is why the Qur'an says: *"We will show them Our manifest signs (proofs) in the horizons of the universe and within their own selves"* (Fussilat 41:53). This is evidence that God has placed in our beings to confirm the truth of an afterlife. We cannot see afterlife here; we can rationally deduce it and feel it with our other faculties.

The One who created us is the Most-Wise and the Most-Compassionate. This world was created to show us the Creator's Attributes. As such, we do not see a single act of creation without wisdom and mercy. If we are invited to a house, and the owner has prepared for us nice food, comfortable space and all that we need and enjoy, would we conclude that the owner is a bad person? We have all the evidence in the universe that He is Wise, Merciful, knows our needs and desires, and He provides them. As we get old, the burden of life gets heavier and heavier. We feel our weakness and poverty more than ever. So the Creator is telling us that He is preparing for us a world free of burden.

We must tell our self: Who brought us here? Whoever brought us here has prepared everything for us. We are sure because we experience them. As soon as we are born, our mother's breasts are full of nutritious milk for us. We have no power to ask for it, to claim it, yet it is ready. We are showered by our parents' compassion. If they ignore us (by using their partial-freewill and covering their mirror not to reflect God's Attributes such as the All-Compassionate), other people see us and cannot help but show compassion to us. In a way, God shows us that he is the One who gave us the best treatment as a baby, and He is the one who will take us from here. He turns us into a baby (in need of help) again as we get older, and then takes us back again out of compassion. Why are we happy when He brings us here, but rebel when the same One takes us?

Whoever creates life creates death. Life and death are both meaningful. Life and death are both purposefully created. Because of our *gaflah* (heedlessness, indolence), not realizing the reality of our life here, we do not think that the One who brought us here is giving death to us. Yet we mistakenly view death as the lack of something (life). This is our misperception. When someone gives us money, we become immediately happy and exclaim, "What perfect timing! This gift was given when I most needed it." God's actions, while I had the glasses, were compassionate and wise. Since birth, we have been constantly showered with blessings. Yet we think of life as our own possession and live as if it was not given to us. We do not heed the Giver. In fact, we cannot even say "I live." I am made to live, I am given this life. Can we claim any of our faculties? We are not even aware of how and when we were given them. So when he is taking back the glasses, I cannot say that God is punishing me. This is a misperception and it is disrespectful to the One who gives us the gift and is replacing it with a better gift! God is still Compassionate and Wise as He was when He blessed us with our life. We do not see anything in creation that is meaningless or lacks wisdom. In *Ayat al-Kursi* (al-Baqarah 2:255), it is mentioned that God does not fall asleep even for a split second. Have we seen the universe not functioning properly even for a split second? Any neglect in creation? So we are wrong to interpret the "creation of death" as bad.

Through worship and belief, we make our lives meaningful and get ready to face death. Belief means realizing that whoever brought me here is wise and compassionate. Death is not annihilation. Death is a deliberate creation. We need to train our understanding to realize that death is creation. When a baby is born, everyone visiting congratulates the family. The same, however, does not happen when someone dies, because God has created us not to like death for a purpose as well. Our dislike of death and nonexistence causes us to hope for eternity.

There is a very conscious order in this world making us realize why we are here. Everything is a message-bearer. It carries a message from the Transcendent One. Belief and worship teaches us God's Attributes and render us happy about the world to come.

We can talk about many signs/evidences for the existence of the afterlife. The first one is the Messengers. In the history of humankind there have always been Messengers. They have all given the news of the afterlife; that we will be taken there according to the Creator's promises. The first Prophet was Adam, peace be upon him. It is beautiful that the first man was a Prophet. All of us are descendants of a Prophet! The first promise of eternity can be found in scripture and in the Prophets' message. And the second promise of eternity is placed within us: our desire for eternity. Yet, wrong-doers do not want to believe in the afterlife because they do not want to be held accountable for their actions. Evidence of resurrection occurs constantly in this world. Yesterday is gone; today is new. The last minute is gone and this minute is created. Trees die in the fall, but are resurrected in the spring.

Perceiving death as a burden/evil is our mistake. The source of a burden is in our attitude of arrogance and ignorance. We must acknowledge our reality of being created by the One who is absolutely compassionate.

For example, asking for forgiveness, in a sense, relieving ourselves of arrogance, is a source of happiness. It relaxes us, which is why *salam* means peace and submission: They are corollaries of each other. Our expectations may not be the same with God's plans, so our desires may not come true because God did not appoint our desires as the engineer of this universe (and thank God for that!). After we confirm (*tasdiq*) that He is indeed the All-Wise, the All-Compassionate, we submit our mind and desires to the will of God. Asking for forgiveness is itself belief and brings inner-peace, and only someone who submits to God is blessed with the humbleness to ask for forgiveness.

The hope for paradise (i.e. for God's mercy) contains paradise in itself: This very feeling brings instantaneous inner-peace (i.e. Paradise). If we sincerely believe that God is merciful, we ask for forgiveness and ask for paradise. Paradise is in the seed of belief. Unbelievers, who do not believe in God, are waiting to die and go to nonexistence. This is living hell, here and now. Thus, everyone builds and begins living their paradise and hell in this life. Belief in the compassionate and wise Creator is living paradise, and faith in chaos an meaningless life is a hellish state of mind and heart.

6. Belief in Destiny (*Qadar*)

Partial-Freewill (*Iradah al-Juz'iyyah*)

Say (to the believers): "Whether you keep secret what is in your bosoms or reveal it, God knows it. He knows whatever is in the heavens and whatever is on the earth. God has full power over everything. (Al Imran 3:29)

...It may well be that you dislike a thing but it is good for you, and it may well be that you love a thing but it is bad for you. God knows, and you do not know. (al Baqarah, 2:216)

When we are talking about destiny and using words which are used in the other Abrahamic faiths, one thing to keep in mind is this: Sometimes they might mean the same thing in Islam and Christianity but the content might be different. Destiny (*qadar*) means Divine measure, determination, and judgment in creation of things, to predetermine or preordain everything. Divine Decree (*qada*) means to implement or to put into effect what has been predetermined.

To give an example, it is predetermined for me to write this page. God has the knowledge of this beforehand, which is destiny. Writing these words at this moment is Divine Decree implementing what has been predetermined. So Divine Decree is the things predetermined actually taking place. The extent of God's knowledge is explained in the following Qur'anic verse:

> With Him are the keys of the Unseen; none knows them but
> He. And He knows whatever is on the land and in the sea; not
> a leaf falls but He knows it; neither is there a grain in the dark
> layers of earth, nor anything green or dry, but is (recorded) in
> a Manifest Book. (al-An'am 6:59)

Since God is beyond time and space, and since everything is included in His knowledge, He encompasses the past, present, and the future as one point. He knows everything before they are created by Him. No analogy or comparison would be sufficient to explain this concept since our perception is so limited.

If everything has been predetermined, where does freewill come into all this? Partial-freewill is included in Destiny; they are not mutually exclusive. We do not do something because God recorded it (predetermined it); God knew beforehand what we would do. Yet again using the past tense in reference to God is meaningless since time is nothing but God continuing to create. Time does not have a substantial or real existence. Hence pre-determination (God's knowledge of what was, what is, and what will be) does not contradict with partial-freewill. The following analogy helps illustrate the point: You are on top of a hill overlooking a plateau (flat terrain) on which there is a straight road. A car is speeding really fast on the road. Because you are on top of the hill, you can see that there is a barricade on the road. The driver cannot see that. Because of your position, and the fact that you see the barricade, you know that the car will hit the barricade. Eventually, the car does hit the barricade. You knew beforehand that the car was going to hit the barricade. But the car did not hit the barricade because you knew it.

Partial-freewill is crucial in the overall scheme of creation. The purpose of creation is for us to know and to love God by contemplating His revelations (scriptures and the creation) and following His guidance. This constitutes our education (including the trials and examination) in this life. Only if we have the potential to choose can we be held accountable for our actions. Otherwise, there would be no point for us to be created or no logic in us being judged on the Day of Judgment (being judged means that we will face our reality: Whatever mental/spiritual state we arrived in this life, we will be resurrected with that state). We deserve punishment for our own wrong decisions/thoughts/actions. Or we will receive eternal happiness through God's grace if we follow God's guidance: seek to submit and have inner peace. Therefore, freewill plays a crucial role in enabling us to choose and therefore be responsible for our actions.

Now how much can we actually choose? We only have partial freewill. The first and obvious opposition is birth. We have absolutely no say in where we are born and what type of parents we have, and these factors may play a big role in determining our life trajectory. Just like birth, there is other things in our life that we cannot control.

It is as if there is a certain plot or a framework into which God places us. I was born in Turkey to Muslim parents, but someone else might have been born in China. Our circumstances are not the same; therefore we will not be judged with the same criteria. We will be judged according to our circumstances. One of God's Divine Attributes is the Most-Just, and perfect justice requires such treatment.

As there are things we cannot choose, we still can make many choices in life with our partial-freewill. Perhaps you may have seen movies where there are two plots within one movie. There is a breaking point where the actor makes a choice and depending on that decision, the rest of the movie unfolds in a certain way. Then they go back and show the actor choosing the other option and the movie unfolds to reveal the alternative plot. In a way, partial-freewill works this way.

We make a choice and God creates the path we choose to walk on. By using our partial-freewill we can potentially rise higher than angels, or go below the level of animals in our spirituality and relationship with God. God guides us to good things and actions, and allows us to use our willpower (*iradah*) to choose the good. I picture our situation as follows: We are moving forward on a path that leads to the prize (inner peace/heaven here and in the afterlife). Both sides of the road are blocked with buffers and road signs warning us not to go off the road and the dangers that would befall. So all the carrots and sticks are there to make sure we stay on the right path. We must exert extra, purposeful effort to go off the road, which leads us to danger (we harm our self by doing so). In this scenario, when we stay on the right path, it is hard to claim any credit to our self! Everything is provided to make sure we do not go astray (hence we say it is by God's grace that we find inner peace/heaven here and in the afterlife). Yet, when we go astray by ignoring all the messages and guides that God continuously places in our life, we know for sure that we are the sole responsible...

Our partial-freewill is included in Divine Will and Destiny. Our relation with Divine Will differs from that of other beings, for only we are given partial-freewill. Based on His knowledge of how we will act and speak, God has recorded all details of our life. He is not bound by our choices, and therefore, past, present, and future. What we consider predetermination exists in relation to us, not to God Himself. For God, predetermination means His eternal knowledge of our acts.

Belief in Destiny is essential because our self-conceit leads us to attribute our accomplishments and good deeds to our self. However, the Qur'an explicitly states that *"While it is God Who has created you and all that you do?"* (as-Saffat 37:96). It is from God's grace that He guides us to good deeds and it is He who creates them. On the other hand, we like to deny responsibility for our sins by ascribing them to Destiny. Did you ever realize how people react differently to events: I got an A vs. the teacher gave me a C! However, God does not like such bad acts, so the accountability belongs to us.

Pre-Determination

How are we going to submit to God's decree, which is destiny? Belief in destiny is one of the pillars of faith in Islam, which is to believe that everything is God's predetermination. The word determining may be problematic because it reminds us of a philosophic school of thought known as determinism, referring to natural determinism. When we talk about destiny, it means Divine determination.

Kitabu mubin is an expression used in the Qur'an and interpreted by Nursi as the explicit form of God's knowledge in this world. Another term used in discussing destiny is *Imamu mubin* or *Lawhi mahfuz*, which literally means "the preserved tablet." This term refers to eternal knowledge of God. As far as our perception of creation is concerned, pre-eternal knowledge means the One who created this universe obviously knew before He created it. He has pre-knowledge of what He will do. Yet it is crucial to understand that even the term pre-knowledge is from our perspective, not from God's perspective, because we perceive things in time. There is no past, present or future for God.

The Qur'an states that things in any form are inscribed in a clear book. We can find the traces of knowledge which proves that the One who creates things knows beforehand. If we look at the creation, we will see the signs illustrating that everything is known before it is created. A perfect example would be the seed of a tree that preserves in it the plan of the tree, or the human DNA that contains their genetic code.

Everything is determined before it comes into existence, during its existence, and after it passes. We understand that things are determined during their creation since we observe that creation is taking place through absolute knowledge. We witness that the Creator knows what He is doing (everything is orderly, purposeful, etc.). What is more is that it is determined, or preserved before and after.

When something is happening in this world, are we really sure that the Creator knows it or does it just happen? Say, I "accidently" drop and break my glasses. I did not know that they would break before it happened. Is it also the case with the Creator? No. The One who creates "the breaking of my glasses" knows it beforehand. It means that it is within His knowledge. Whoever is creating the action, knows it will happen. So if we know who is purposefully creating the event, and that He knows it would happen, then we start to evaluate everything accordingly. If we know that what happened is in His knowledge who is the Most-Just, the Most-Compassionate and the All-Knowing, our reaction changes. For instance, we do not curse when our glasses "accidently" break. We pose and contemplate why God is creating this event, because we know that nothing is "accidental."

We do not know what will happen five minutes later. If we know that creation is known by the Creator before and after, it changes our perception of everything. It will make a great difference in our life to know that the Creator knew it before and knows it after. If we know that the Creator is infinitely compassionate, then we would see the compassion in whatever happens to us. It is happening to me deliberately by a Merciful Sustainer, Designer. Therefore, these two perspectives are completely contradictory.

Depending on how we "know" the Creator, and our awareness that all is coming from a Most Compassionate Creator, we would understand that whatever is happening with us is coming purposefully from the will of the Most Compassionate One. We "know" that the Creator is the All-Wise and the All-Compassionate by reading the Qur'an and observing the creation. I witness that this Creator never does something unwise or in vain. Only after going through this confirmation (*tasdiq*; the Qur'anic *iman* education), when something that I do not like happens to me, I would not rebel saying "Why is it happening to me?" With this perspective the world would become unbearable for us. The more we are aware that all is under the control of the Wise and Compassionate Creator, the more relaxed we would become in our daily lives.

Divine determining refers to the Divine—God is determining. Depending on our understanding of God, it has a positive connotation. God does not tyrannize His creatures. Why would He have created us anyway to torture or harm? Do we make a computer to break or smash it afterwards?

There is no evidence or sign of despotism in the creation. Some people, whatever they are living through, they see nothing but torture and suffering. But the negative things that happen to us are a result of our negative perceptions and misuse of our partial-freewill and covering our mirror not to reflect the manifestations of God's Attributes, and people want to accept that they are the source of the mistakes.

We cannot just say "because God says so." The Qur'an urges us to turn to the creation in order to confirm the revelation, because creation, the revelation, and the Prophets say the same thing. Still, some people may say: "I do not experience what the revelation says." Then, we must check ourselves, and see why we don't perceive things the way the revelation explains. There may be something wrong with our perception. The verse explains that God never hurts or oppresses His creatures, but His creatures harm themselves. Take an example from the creation—sunlight. The suns rays are full of dangerous elements, yet it gets filtered through the ozone layer and only the beneficial rays reach us. However, we have damaged the ozone layer, so it is not able to filter the sunlight as it was intended to do. How can we claim that God is harming us when we, with our freewill, harm ourselves?

Have we ever observed anything in the creation that is out of order? God says in the Qur'an: *"We have created everything in pairs"* (adh-Dhariyat 51:49). The first example of this that comes to mind is the creation of man and woman. As if the pot and the pot lid are both there but created separately; when we put them together, they complement each other perfectly. Even if they have been developed in different conditions and in different places, they are perfect for each other.

Everything is in perfect balance. The structure of the planets and the atoms are exactly the same. They are both in perfect balance.

If after observing this perfect order and balance, we still see something wrong, we must turn to ourselves and ask: "Why do I see it this way? Am I looking at this the wrong way?" When we lose something, we get furious. We do not want to admit that we are to blame. If you put your keys in a place and do not touch them, they stay there forever. They cannot get lost on their own. Yet we do not want to admit our mistakes. If we do not like something, we blame other things rather than us. If I burn myself, I blame the fire; I do not blame myself even though I have used my freewill wrongly and brought the harm to myself.

God creates things with differentiation, making everything different than the other. No human being resembles the other. They have been made different deliberately. So whoever created this world completely knows what He is doing. Nothing is exactly identical to another thing. The Creator has a deliberate choice in everything He creates. When we understand this, it strengthens our willpower (*iradah*) and conscience to silence our ego/*nafs* when it attributes God's Attributes to itself (i.e. I know, I did a good job, etc.). We can tell our *nafs* "You are wrong; the Creator definitely knows what He is doing." If we are convinced that the Creator knows what He is doing, then we check ourselves. This is a fight between the human being and his *nafs*. We think that we are fighting with God.

If we do not heed the revelation or pay attention to the signs in the creation, the fight between us and the ego/*nafs* goes on around the clock. But as we begin to get educated and transformed by the revelation, we are able to silence the whisperings of the *nafs*.

The Qur'an does not give information or list facts. It educates us. The Prophet performed the Daily Prayers five times a day within the community for more than 15 years. After his death, the community still could not agree on how exactly he prayed. This means there was no focus on how it was done. It is a very important pillar of Islam, but he did not instruct the people how to do it. From this we understand that the core of the teaching of religion is not the do's and don'ts. If we listen to the Qur'an as much as we heed the news on TV, we would learn and practice the path of submission. It is not information; it is training and education. The Qur'an says, "*...believe and do good...*" (al-Baqarah 2:25). However, we have something inside of us (ego/*nafs*) that tries to keep us from doing good.

Nafs is the personal representative of Satan in our life. If we give importance to it, it reigns over our feelings, thoughts, and decisions. Our fight should be to blame the *nafs* rather than the Creator when we face something we do not like. Our own wrong interpretation of the event results in harm. We have been given partial-freewill: If we cut our finger, it is our mistake. We cannot blame God or the causes He has created, like the sharp knife. Our duty is to train our self to realize how God is creating everything in balance, in a perfect way. When we confirm this, it becomes more and more difficult to conclude that "the entire universe is in perfect balance and order, yet in this small event of me cutting my finger, God has not created compassion and balance." After looking at the evidence in the universe and confirming that God is the All-Compassionate and the All-Wise, then we would trust in the Creator that He never makes a mistake nor harms any of His creatures. Observing the universe to find evidence in the creation is the method of the Qur'an (*usul*). First we observe the creation; then we confirm that the revelation is absolutely right.

So is being created with this *nafs* a punishment for the human beings? Having a *nafs* is not a fault in our creation. It is purposefully given to us by God and its creation is perfect. But we are infected with the materialistic philosophy of this age, which does not accept God's Wisdom and Compassion but attributes everything to "nature" or to "chance." We have been taught and poisoned not to see the purpose behind creation. Yet our minds and hearts beg answers about the meaning of life and sink deeper and deeper without fulfilling this need for meaning. Only when we heed the teachings of the Prophets and strive to be trained/educated by their message do we find some solace. Anyone can see that there is an apple on the table (as positivist science simply describes), but why is there an apple (why has it been created?) and what do I do with it (how to relate to the creation and how to use it)? The real teaching is how to be the agent of God on earth, how to control ourselves and reach our highest potential. This is true education (*tarbiyah*). Everything we do must be in the name of the Creator. Belief then is the indispensable component of our education. Without belief, our actions have no importance. We would keep praying while also criticizing God. We would continue to be unhappy with God's creation, our life, and all that happens to us. Yet, *iman* and stress/depression cannot exist in the same heart, at the same time.

Although belief in destiny seems to be a theoretical issue, it has many practical implications in our daily life. It is to practice our faith in our life. In recent centuries, Muslims have been over-emphasizing practice and jurisprudence/*fiqh* at the expense of belief and theology.

Islamic scholars have begun to concentrate on jurisprudence/*fiqh* and the practical side of worship, because it is concrete and not open to much discussion. Decisions on these issues were based on the Qur'an, the *sunnah* (actions and sayings of Prophet Muhammad), and the consensus of the scholars or analogy method. The rules outlined in the blessed Qur'an are marvelous. The inheritance law is prescribed in half a page of the Qur'an, and out of this half page, scholars wrote volumes of books on inheritance law. In other words, the Qur'an is so concise that it summarizes these volumes in half a page. Yet in the Qur'an, only about 280 verses are related to practice, and about 6350 verses are related to faith and the meaning of our existence. This should make us rethink the relative importance of faith and practice.

The Qur'anic *iman* education is difficult. There are no easily achieved and tangible results that you can "show off." You may spend years and years and may not see any results. Moreover, matters related to belief are not concrete as they are open to debate. If I go through spiritual training for years, my children have to start from scratch for themselves. However with rules on practice, I study and write them down, my children have to only read and apply them as dictated. Or I do not even have to study the rules myself; for others have studied and recorded them, so when I need them in my practical life, I refer to them. It is far more challenging with *iman* education. The more you learn faith, the more humble you become. The *nafs* fights to keep up its arrogant reign. To study religion from the perspective of belief is difficult.

When we are becoming more interested in "religion," we tend to start adopting the do's and don'ts faster than we comprehend the meaning behind these rules. In other words, we find it easier to dress more modestly or give to charity, then to give up our ego's false pride, false claims to ownership of our qualities, feelings, success, beauty, kids, etc. Hence, we end up with many "observant" people who are not more humble, peaceful, relaxed, etc.

Islam (submission) is a *din*/path/religion, which educates us to live by our faith. Belief in destiny means we put our belief in practice. If we want to live according to our belief in God, this is the subject of belief in destiny. If we want to live according to our belief in God, in angels, in the afterlife, in the revelations and in the Messengers, this can only be done through our belief in destiny. Belief in destiny is an aspect of belief which covers all other pillars of faith, and itself has no object. You believe in the angels, the object is the angels. You believe in the afterlife, the object is the afterlife. You believe in destiny, what is the object of destiny? Nothing. It means you believe in destiny, you live accordingly. The object of destiny is living according to your belief in God and angels... etc. In our daily life, when things happen to us, we react, perceive and interpret them according to our belief in all the pillars. This is the belief in destiny. In Islam (the path of submission), what makes one a *muslim* (submitter) is not the ritual practice. It is our belief in God and our way of living according to our belief. You treat the things around you according to your belief that everything is represented by angels, that there are angels everywhere. In conclusion, "I believe in destiny" means, "I believe everything is from God."

Part III: Worship

Confirmation by Action

We said that Islam means to surrender to God's will, and a *muslim* is one who surrenders. So how can we surrender to God's will? Simply, by trying to live "There is no deity but God" and by giving God's property to God (thus everything). As we embark upon our quest to find answers to our existential questions, we soon realize that we do not possess anything. What we have is His property given to us as a trust.

We learn how to surrender from the teachings of the Creator. God's compassion and wisdom entails not leaving us without guidance. The universe is like a book, and in order to be able to learn its message, we need to learn its alphabet. For this reason, God sent us teachers and guidebooks that explain how to surrender to the truth. By surrendering to God we accept our servanthood, which brings us to the concept of worship in Islam. Worship is a very comprehensive concept in Islam, which literally means living in servanthood.

Everything one does can be considered worship if it is done with the consciousness that we are servants of God. Work, study, sports, sleep, marriage, cleaning the home, and everything in our life can be transformed into worship If it is done with a servanthood consciousness, nothing is from me and I am only a mirror that can reflect God's Attributes. All is bad if I choose not to reflect the goodness. All my actions are a prayer to Him asking for the outcome: My actions are my active prayer. Cooking is but a prayer for a meal that is created by God and a result of my active prayer. Conceived this way, life becomes a continuous cycle of prayer, thankfulness and repentance.

The topics we will discuss in the following pages, such as Daily Prayers, fasting and almsgiving, are essentially tools to help us surrender, prescribed to the created by the Creator who knows us better than we know ourselves.

Purpose of Creation

Or did you think that We created you in vain (so that you should devote all your time to play and entertainment), and that you would not be brought back to Us? (al-Mu'minun 23:115)

Why was I created? What am I to do with my life? Why did God send Prophets? Human beings have always been intrigued by these questions since their answers are critical to unearth numerous other mysteries. Moreover, the purpose of creation even helps explain issues related to the afterlife such as what will become of us when we die. In other words, the goal of creation is the goal of life.

There are several verses in the Qur'an outlining very clearly why God created the universe and humankind. God was the only existence, and He wanted to be known and loved by conscious beings who, unlike the angels, would have the freewill to choose to worship/acknowledge God. Thus, God created the universe in which the human beings would dwell, multiply, and go through a lifelong trial till Judgment Day when the universe would be destroyed only to turn into a different realm for the Hereafter.

The human mind has the intellectual capacity to reach the conclusion that for the complexity of creation to exist in such an orderly manner, there has to be a Creator. But how can we know the reason why God created the universe, and in particular, humankind? Islam recognizes four sources to find the answers: the Messengers, the scriptures, human conscience, and the universe as "the book of signs." These sources explain that everything in the creation manifest God's Attributes in order for us to know, to love, and to worship God.

The Arabic word *khalq* comes from the root *kh-l-q* and refers to the act of creation. Creation in Islamic terminology primarily signifies creating something from nothingness in accordance with the creatio ex nihilo (the doctrine of the theory of creation from nothingness). The ability to create belongs only to God, who is the Al-Khaliq. He is the one who creates from nothing, "establishing at the same time the states, conditions, and the sustenance of all that He has created."[10]

Islam is built on the principal of God's unity (*tawhid*), which is prevalent in every aspect and practice of the religion. Since He is the only Creator, the entire universe owes its existence to God; therefore He is the only one worthy of worship. Likewise, all Islamic principals are deduced by reason and are built on each other and can be traced back to the fact that God is the sole Creator.

The Creator "not only has created but also governs the world according to an order that issues from His Wisdom as well as His Will."[11] Thus, God's hand is present in all things at all times as is evident in the harmony and order of nature. The Qur'anic verse, *"Say: 'In Whose Hand is the absolute ownership and dominion of all things...'"* (al-Mu'minun 23:88) explains this phenomenon clearly. Everything in the cosmos has a Divine aspect because God breathed His Divine Breath into it. As described by Nasr, Ibn Arabi states that "there is no property in the cosmos without a Divine support and a lordly attribute"[12] and that "The very essence of cosmos is the 'Breath of Compassionate' (*nafas ar-Rahman*) while cosmic forms and all that constitutes the order of nature emanate from the archetype realities and ultimately the Divine Essence Itself."[13]

Thus, Islam views all animate and inanimate creatures as sacred beings that reflect the manifestations of God's Attributes. Environmentalism and humanism (in the sense of loving human beings because of the Creator) are innate to Islam due to this principal, and are manifest

---

[10] Bayrak 2000, p. 64.
[11] Nasr 2000, p. 53.
[12] Nasr 2000, p. 61.
[13] Ibid.

in Islamic literature and the practices of Prophet Muhammad, peace and blessings be upon him.

Islamic theology holds that creation is not without a purpose; rather, it has a Divine purpose. Numerous verses in the Qur'an urge humans to question and observe creation to see that it was not created in vain. God says in the Qur'an:

> We have not created the heavens and the earth and all that is between them in vain (so that people should think themselves at liberty to act each according to his own desires and inclinations). That is the mere conjecture of those who disbelieve. Woe to those who disbelieve because of the Fire! (Sad 38:27)

God's intention in creating the universe is clearly outlined in the Qur'an and is centered on humanity. Numerous verses in the Qur'an explain how the whole universe, heavens and the earth, are arranged to provide for and to serve humanity (al-Baqarah 2:22; 29). Thus the universe and everything within are subordinate to mankind which puts the responsibility on man to take care of nature, bringing us back to the environmentalism theme in Islam.

The universe has another, more essential role to play apart from providing for and serving humanity. Everything in the creation manifests God's Attributes. In other words, the most important trait of the cosmos is its theophany. God has also designed it to be a "book of signs" for humankind. Human beings may recognize God's Majesty and comprehend His Divine Attributes (*Asma al-Husna*) by contemplating nature. As Esposito argues, "nature, properly viewed, becomes a revealed book very much like the Qur'an is itself composed of individual signs or miracles."[14] God says in the Qur'an:

> But do they, then, never observe the sky above them (to ponder Our Knowledge and Power; and reflect) how We have constructed it and adorned it, and that there are no rifts in it? (Qaf 50:6)

---

[14] Esposito 1995, p.474.

When viewed from this perspective, the universe takes on an entirely different meaning and becomes increasingly significant for human beings. The study of natural sciences becomes almost an act of worship since it leads to the knowledge of the Creator. In the verses above, God urges human beings to use the intelligence that He gave them. It is emphasized that we are given this intelligence (and are not created as a plant or an animal with limited intelligence) so that we use it in the right way and get to know God. As early Muslims took up this command, both natural and social sciences flourished in the Muslim world for centuries.

In one of the most well-known phrases on the subject of the purpose of creation, God conveyed through Prophet Muhammad, peace and blessings be upon him: "I was a Hidden Treasure and I loved to be known, and so I created the world."[15] God manifests His Attributes through His creation since He is a transcendent being that cannot be limited to time and space, and cannot be conceived directly. Also, Prophet Muhammad's own words explain that "... the universe and its contents were created in order to make known the Creator, and to make known that good is to praise it."[16]

Both of these *hadith* refer to and require a being with freewill and intelligence to know and praise God, which brings us to the core of the matter: If the universe was created to serve man, then what is the purpose of the creation of humankind? There are three main reasons, agreed upon by a wide range of scholars, as to why God created mankind: to know God, to love God, and to worship God. All of the Prophets, the revealed scriptures and the universe, as the book of signs, serve as tools through which we know God. The reason for their existence is solely to guide humanity to recognize, acknowledge, and revere God as He deserves. Only after knowing God can we begin to love God in a more conscious and appreciative manner. God says in the Qur'an, *"I have not created the jinn and humankind but to (know*

---

[15] Nasr 2000, p. 133.
[16] Lings 1991, p. 1.

and) worship Me (exclusively)" (adh-Dhariyat 51:56). Then the question takes on a new form; what is really meant by serving God, or how does one serve God?

The Arabic word used in this verse is *ibadah* which is translated as 'worship' (origin is 'weorthscipe' which means 'honor'). In this sense, all the Prophets preached *ibadah*, conveying the message of what God wants human beings to do. In general, worship is defined as all those acts within the circle of *halal*[17] (do not have to be physical, even an intention can be counted as worship) done for the sake of God, to please Him.

Why does God want human beings to worship him by obeying Him and His Divine Laws? Without *iman* (faith) in one's heart, the immediate response to obedience and worship is "why does God need my worship?" However, it is the human beings themselves who need the worship. Islam presents Divine Laws (*shari'ah*) that guide all aspects of life by distinguishing right from wrong. As Philips puts it, "The Creator alone knows best what is beneficial for His creation and what is not. The Divine Laws command as well as prohibit various acts and substances to protect human spirit, human body and society from harm. In order for human beings to fulfill their potential by living righteous lives, they need to worship God through obedience to His commandments."[18] Also, the underlying purpose of the regular acts of worship is to remember God constantly.

What follows is the "trial/education"; a concept common in all three monotheistic traditions, though in Islam, it takes a slightly different connotation (al-Kahf 18:7; al-Mulk 67:2). Human beings will be held accountable for every single action they do in this life, the good and the bad. Since God provided humanity with guidelines (the scriptures) and the Messengers, and He gave reason and freewill—

[17] "Circle of *halal*" is a phrase used to signify all those things, acts, and intentions within the boundaries of permissible category in Islam.
[18] Philips, p.3.

without accountability and the Judgment Day, creation would be in vain. God says in the Qur'an:

> He it is Who created the heavens and the earth in six Days —and His Supreme Throne was upon the water—that He might make trial of you to manifest which of you is best in conduct... (Hud 11:7)

> God has created the heavens and the earth in truth (for meaningful purpose, on solid foundations of truth and embodying it), and so that every soul may be recompensed for what it has earned (in this world), and they will not be wronged. (al-Jathiyah 45:22)

Another essential aspect of the creation of humankind lies in the concept of vicegerency (being a representative or agent of God on earth). What does it mean for humanity to be the vicegerent of God on earth?

> We did indeed offer the Trust to the Heavens and the Earth and the Mountains; but they refused to undertake it, being afraid thereof: but man undertook it; he was indeed unjust and foolish. (al-Ahzab 33:72)

As explained in the above verse, God has called upon the whole of creation and informed it that He has a trust to offer. All of creation, including the mountains, refused to accept this challenging trust, except man. Thus, man became God's trustee on earth. There are several clear verses in the Qur'an stating that God has appointed humanity as His vicegerent on earth, *"He it is Who has* appointed you vicegerents on the earth (to improve it and rule over it according to God's commands)..."* (al-An'am 6:165). Philips explains this long term cycle of the role of human beings as follows:

> God created human beings with the potential to be good and evil. He implanted in man the desires that need to be controlled according to the divine law. God created human beings knowing that they would disobey Him. He thus taught them

how to repent and purify themselves. The story of Adam and Eve is a prototype of human beings' repeated cycle. They forgot God's commandment and were lured by Satan. They disobeyed God and afterwards repented and God forgave them.[19]

The Qur'an outlines the conclusions to be drawn after one acknowledges God as the sole Creator. Since God creates and sustains everything, then His creatures are to live according to His Will. Thus, the Messengers and the scriptures expound the right way of life for His creatures. God urges humans to use their reasoning power to contemplate the universe and the scriptures so that they can recognize and acknowledge God's wonders. Awe for and thankfulness to God naturally follows, since our existence depends only upon Him:

> Now O humankind! Worship your Lord Who has created you as well as those before you (and brought you up in your human nature and identity), so that you may attain reverent piety towards Him and His protection (against any kind of straying and its consequent punishment in this world and the Hereafter). (al-Baqarah 2:21)

Since "His being the Creator is a central reason that he is deserving of worship for the entire universe owes its existence to him,"[20] worship is a requirement of loving and acknowledging God. Also, worshiping God "proceeds not merely from his gracious creative act in the past, but from dependence upon him for existence at every instant of the present and the future."[21]

> And what reason do I have that I should not worship Him Who originated me with a nature particular to me, and to Whom you all (as well as I) are being brought back (to give an account of our lives)? (Ya-Sin 36:22)

God urges us to understand our creation so that we can fulfill our purpose of creation. The answer to the crucial question "why are we

---

[19] Ibid.
[20] Esposito 1995, p. 472.
[21] Ibid.

created?" helps unfold numerous other religious and philosophical questions; thus it is an inclusive and important matter to study and comprehend in the context of Islam.

Conclusively, the purpose of creation can be summarized as follows: God was the only Being; He wanted to be known, loved, and worshiped by beings that have the freewill to choose to worship Him. Creation was not a necessity, but the Will of God. Human beings regard life as their most precious gift and would do anything not to lose it. He created us as human beings, even without our knowledge, and He also sustains us and makes it possible for us to enjoy this life. From this perspective, loving and worshiping God becomes more relevant and logical.

"God Has Created Adam in His Image"

The Prophetic saying (*hadith*) "God has created Adam in His image" is a parable that should be understood in terms of attributes, not necessarily in its literal meaning. "...in His image" refers to Divine Attributes rather than appearance. In other words, God has created Adam (human beings) with the capacity to reflect His Attributes of Perfection (*Asma al-Husna*). Thus, each of us is created in the image of God in order to reflect His Attributes from the functional point of view. Likewise, verse 95:4 of the Qur'an states that God has created human in the best form (*ahsan-i taqwem*). God turns our attention to the signs within us and urges us to ponder upon them:

> On the earth there are (clear) signs (of God's Oneness as Lord and Sovereign) for those who seek certainty; And also in your own selves. Will you then not see (the truth)? (adh-Dhariyat 51:20–21)

The parable then, is referring to the signs within us. In light of this Prophetic saying and these verses, can we not say that we are the masterpiece of our Creator, and the signs in us are the manifestations of God's Attributes? In a way, everything in us is created by God, such as our physical body, our senses, and the way we think and behave. As far as our creation is concerned, nothing is missing or imperfect. The Creator has manifested His Attributes in the best way.

What should we make of this reality about our existence? Should we be proud of it and spoil the world with our self-indulgence as if we were its rightful tyrants? Once we realize that we are the masterpiece of the Creator and that we have the potential to manifest His Attributes of perfection, our responsibility is to try to develop this potential and act accordingly without contradicting our true nature/ *fitrah*. When we act, we are to reflect, for instance, His Mercy, and realize that it is not from us, but from God.

Developing our potential does not mean improving it (as if it was not perfect to begin with). We are already given the full potential to reflect all of God's Attributes. Our only responsibility is to avoid covering up (the literal meaning of *kufr*) or preventing God's Attributes from being reflected through us. When we choose not to reflect God's Mercy through us (thus act mercilessly), we are hindering our potential and the purpose of our creation. On the other hand, when we let our potential and purpose manifest themselves, it is from God. In other words, when we help someone in need by complying with our inner call (or acting in the way we have been created), we should realize that we are not the source of this virtue, but only a mirror.

Everyone has been created with different levels of abilities to develop. As Rumi put it beautifully, every cup created by God is full, but some cups are smaller than others. Yet, everyone has the same duty towards his/her Creator: submission. We have been given a certain capacity and our duty is to fill our cup/fulfill our capacity in the way God wants. So what does God want from us? God is educating us through the Scriptures and the Messengers to accept reality as it is. In other words, God wants us to realize and acknowledge that nothing is from us, and that everything is only from Him.

So we have a big responsibility. We are carrying the best "jewels" from the treasure of God's Attributes. If we are not benefiting from them, it does not matter how many years we carry the jewels, but if we use them in the best way, we benefit greatly. Thus, we should not cover them up, or hinder their manifestation through us. We should not claim to own them or use them in a wrong way.

We have been created in the image of God, given the potential to manifest God's Attributes so that we might use them to get to know our Creator. We can know God through our own existence because the Attributes of God are engraved in us. Thus, our duty as human beings is two-fold: knowing and recognizing God and acting accordingly.

Knowing and recognizing God is belief (*iman*); acting accordingly is the action (*amal*). Belief comes first, and action follows. And inevitably, acting without acknowledging the real source of all our qualities leads to arrogance.

Ways Leading to God

... So do not hold yourselves pure (sinless; it is vain self-justification). He knows best him who keeps from disobedience to God in reverence for Him and piety. (an-Najm 53:32)

We have an innate disposition to love and to always defend ourselves. God has given this disposition to defend our rights and to be dignified as a human being. But the ego/*nafs*' job is to claim its independence of the Creator and declare false ownership of our qualities.

Every sense we have been given, we can use them in two opposite ways. We can either use it for the purpose it was given to us, or abuse the feeling and use it for the *nafs*. Through *iman* education we can direct our senses to the positive ways.

The ego loves only itself, and sacrifices everything for itself. He considers himself worthy of worship. He exonerates himself from any fault, looks for any excuse to disclaim any fault. The verse is specifically referring to a person's introspective analysis in which he sees himself as faultless. In a way, God is saying "do not consider yourself pure, do not justify yourself, do not find excuses, do not exonerate yourself." We need to realize that our *nafs* has such an inclination, hence with this awareness, when that inclination arises in us, we do not let it overtake our *iradah* (willpower), and we do not act upon it.

Our creation, including our partial-freewill and the *nafs*, is perfect. To have *nafs* is not bad, but to follow our *nafs* is bad. Because of our *nafs*, we can say *la ilaha*. We realize through our ego: "I do not want to worship something that is not worthy of worship." We swim against the current of the ego to gain strength and rise in spiritual ranks. What makes us human beings (i.e. our difference from animals and other created beings) is our partial-freewill, our capacity to reason and *nafs*. Choice necessitates alternatives, one correct and one wrong, true vs. false, white vs. black. If I want to, I can choose the false, but I do not have to. *Nafs* is always telling us to choose the false. But *nafs* has no power over us. If we educate our self through *iman*, then *nafs* loses its influence. Gradually, the *nafs* realizes it is pointless to suggest the falsehood to the person. Then we become the perfect/complete person (*al-insan al-kamil*), by becoming a perfect worshipper of God, *abd*.

Is feeding the poor necessarily a good deed/action? It depends! If the deed is done with the realization that it is my Creator who gave me the capacity to help someone, I am only a mirror reflecting the manifestations of His Attributes. A person whose ego says: "I am feeding you," as if claiming "I am your Lord," like the Pharaohs, is in fact increasing his arrogance through this seemingly good deed. The person who feeds someone and recognizes the Creator as the source of that ability is living in pure submission. So in a sense, we could outwardly look like the best human being in terms of actions, but without submission to God, we would be pure ego, and our actions would be void, having no value in reality. When there is *shirk* (associating partners with God) in our actions, our actions become void. Shirk is committed by not attributing the action to God, but appropriating it to ourselves, as if we are the source of the goodness.

When the sunlight is reflecting from a mirror, the mirror is not the source of the light. Likewise, we are not the source of goodness. But when we close that mirror, preventing the light from reflecting, this is our fault. We choose to prevent the light. Hence, we are the cause of the bad we choose.

The Role of Intellect and Heart

We have been given numerous faculties/qualities: intellect/ reason, heart, sense, ego, conscience, partial-freewill, willpower, etc. When we make decisions, we use all these faculties simultaneously. We may think that we think and choose solely with our intellect, but so many other faculties play a role in each decision.

Our intellect looks at the apparent face of creation through the five external senses that collect information. For instance, when we see a tea cup, we say, "There is a cup and there is tea in it." We observe and tell what is apparently there. But we like the tea; we enjoy the taste; we feel sorry for those who do not have it; we want to share it with those who are in need of it... etc. Thus, actions we take have many reasons behind them, not only reason.

The plant grows as if the cells are reproducing themselves. Yes, this is true, but at the end it comes out as an extraordinarily amazing system. Although at first glance, when we observe creation it seems straightforward, all is going on smoothly. Cells multiply; the world revolves around itself. When we look at things carefully, all is precisely measured. The outcome of the precise angle of the worlds axis is amazing. Millions of events are attached to it and they are purposefully designed this way. Then our reason questions what this is and interprets it. While reason tries to interpret it, other human faculties enter this thinking process.

What does the heart entail? Having a heart means consciousness, emotions, senses, being considerate, wanting to help other people even strangers. When our expectations are fulfilled, we are pleased. If I see something I do not like, I wish it was not so. For example, we ask our sick friend to get well soon. This is not a rational desire. If he could get well soon on his own, he would not have been sick to begin with. So a greeting of "get well soon" expresses our hopes, although rationally, we know that to make the apparent system of creation help our friend to "get well" is not within our capacity. Our senses take us beyond the system of creation to its Creator. The system does not listen to me; it has no conscience, but our feelings require a conscious addressee. This leads us to the Conscious Creator of the system.

When we question whether the heart leads our intellect or vice versa, the matter becomes complicated. Reason looks at the causal relationship. On the other hand, the emotions do not concentrate on the casual relationship. The heart hopes and wishes. It gets frightened. Its limits are completely different than the limits of our intellect.

Let's say I have $100. Using reason, I can only buy three or four books with this money, but my heart wishes for so much more. It wants, for example, to feed all the poor. In the apparent causal relationship, there are no means to do so with what I have, but the heart still desires. I desire that no one hurt each other, that there be no wars, etc.

There is then a contradiction between reason and heart. They do not exclude each other, yet reason is very limited, whereas the heart seems to have no limits. While the heart hopes for infinity in everything, there is no absolute in creation. Everything we observe is limited, bound by time and space. Nothing in this creation that we observe or experience is unlimited. Hence, reason sees the limitations and measures them, while the heart hopes for infinite happiness and beauty. The heart is the mirror of the Divine Attributes. The heart is the mirror of Rab (The Sustainer/Educator/Caretaker). The heart always looks beyond the causal network. It wishes for everything good, but eternally. The heart is one of our faculties that opens up to the Divine sphere. When we engage in retrospective thought and try to analyze what it means for our heart to hope for eternity, we realize that eternity is in the Divine sphere. When we listen to our senses, we see that we desire eternal justice, peace and beauty. Even if we may not be able to describe what they are, we still wish for them. So human senses address that which is beyond the limits of this creation. Even if our senses cannot see any means to realize it, to make it come true, our heart still wants it. There seems to be an apparent contradiction between what we see in this world and what we desire.

What my heart desires is not confirmed by what my intellect can see and can perceive. Since we cannot experience and confirm this desire for eternity, where did it come from? We can conclude that whoever made me gave me these senses, which looks for something beyond the limits of this creation. These desires are innate; we are programmed this way. Everyone dies, everything perishes. But we still want eternity.

"I wish" is the heart; "I know I cannot" is the reason. Reason blocks the heart's path to deciphering the meaning in creation, because reason functions with causal relationships.

How can we utilize reason to help the heart and vice versa? Reason will say "I have this much food," but the heart wants to share it with the hungry. This feeling is given to us as a promise, to understand that this desire will be fulfilled. We see this is a transient world, and our desires cannot be satisfied here. How can this feeling be a promise for eternity? We see in our lives that the Creator always keeps His promises. The babies desire to walk and to speak, and those abilities gradually come. Whatever is promised to them is gradually realized. We have to train our reasoning with the help of the heart.

For example, Prophet Abraham, peace be upon him, was searching for the Creator and started to exercise his reason with the help of his heart. He observed and concluded with his reason that this amazing creation cannot happen accidentally in this perfect way. In a way, his heart was saying: "Yes you are right; look for the one who gives you all these senses, desires, and get to know the Creator of this universe, who is unlimited, and try to see His signs in creation."

In materialist science there is only room for reason. Materialist scientists deny the desires of the heart. For example, for our desire to live eternally and the existence of an eternal Afterlife, they conclude "It cannot happen, it is only human imagination." Billions of people have the same imagination then? This desire for eternity is innate in us, and has been placed in us purposefully. We take the message we receive through the heart, and give another dimension to the cause and effect relationship observed with the reason. The heart tries to understand the meaning. The Creator is giving us a message, a clue about Himself. If the Creator whose creation we observe creates the human being from one cell or a tree out of a tiny seed, then He is revealing His Attributes, He can create everything out of simple things. He can create endless things. The heart is the seed of our desires. Out of this seed, as a response to this prayer, the Creator is creating the eternal life. We cannot see the truth without the heart. Without the help of the heart, the reason cannot reach the truth. Materialist science does not take the message of the heart into account. Belief without reason is also not desired.

How did we invent our wishes? The heart has a letter from God promising He will give all that we desire. Here, in this world, there are free samples of everything. The desire for eternity is a need like hunger; and just like all our physical needs are satisfied here, our desire for eternity will also be satisfied.

Our intellect is only one of the many faculties that make us who we are. Although we know that our parents are there (intellect), we go to visit them because we miss them (heart). We do not always act with our reason. Only reason causes hopelessness, arrogance and selfishness. Reason finds out this world is limited, and concludes that it wants all for itself. Colonialism, wars, power struggles, civilizations dominating the world are all a result of letting the reason dominate our being. On the other hand, the heart realizes its poverty and weakness. It hopes his friend gets well but does not claim "I will give health." This realization is the door opening to God.

Thanksgiving (*Shukr*)

*A*lhamdulillah (all praise is due to God) is the first phrase of the opening chapter of the Qur'an. Thus, the Qur'an's teaching starts with this phrase. It is so significant that it needs to be studied in depth and paid utmost attention. In *Isarat'ul I'jaz* (Signs of Miraculousness), Nursi starts by asserting that if we want to be educated by the Qur'an, we have to start with *alhamdulillah*, understand its meaning, and live accordingly. Praising God is like a concise way of worship: all forms of worship summarized in one phrase. Whatever we praise, we worship.

God created creation for human beings to know Him, *marifatullah*. First, knowledge of God is needed, followed by praise/love of God, followed by worship of God. If we know our God, and if what we know is really God, than we praise Him, and worship Him. From the other way around, if we praise God that means we worship Him; if we worship Him that means we know our God. This is not a distinct separation between worship and praise, yet they are not synonymous either. *Hamd* (praise) is not *ubudiyyah* (servanthood), but praise is the beginning of servanthood that leads us to servanthood. If we are praising something, that is the object of worship, thus we need to be careful of what we praise at all times. Sometimes we say, we are convinced of God's existence, and we believe in Him, and perform our formal worship, yet we praise something other than God. In this case, we are not worshipping God, and we may be conceived as worshipping the thing we praise. We cannot praise the beauty of a flower without directing that praise to its Maker, by remembering (*thikr*) and saying *Subhanallah* or *Masha'Allah*.

The purpose and aim of the universe is for human beings to acquire the knowledge of God. Creation exists for us to reach the knowledge of God. Since the Qur'an starts with the phrase *alhamdu-lillah*, it infers that the ultimate aim of the Qur'an is to teach people to realize that the ultimate aim of creation is praise, leading to knowledge and worship of God. The Qur'an also teaches us how to praise and whom to praise. God says in the Qur'an *"I have not created the jinn and humankind but to (know and) worship Me (exclusively)"* (adh-Dhariyat 51:56). When we praise something in creation, it is to announce its perfections, thus acknowledging its Creator's perfection.

Man is created as a summary or an index of the universe. God put in human beings qualities that manifest God's Attributes. So I can communicate with the universe through the Attributes of the Creator. Since all the universe manifests God's Attributes and I have this quality in me also, I communicate with the universe through the Attributes. This is explained in the second chapter of the Qur'an, which begins with relating the story of Adam's creation.

God taught "the names" to Adam. What is meant by the names in this event is not merely the names of things as generally understood. It is referring to God's Attributes (*Asma al-Husna*). The difference between angels and the human is that each angel manifests only one name of God, whereas human beings manifest all of the Divine Attributes. Each angel receives one command and represents/carries that command here in creation, so each angel manifests one of God's Attributes. Yet the human being can gauge all the commands. So Adam was taught all of God's Attributes. This is why the human being is the *khalif*/representative/agent of God on earth. Also, human beings are given the capacity to perceive all the Attributes of God in creation. Thus, by definition no one can claim to not know God. When we read the book of the universe, we are reading all the meanings that the Creator of this universe intended to convey to us.

The spirit of the human being is coming directly from God: *"When I have fashioned him (in due proportion) and breathed into him of My spirit, fall ye down in obeisance unto him"* (al-Hijr 15:29 and Sad

38:72). This essence of the human being is very significant. The whole creation is also so significant, that in each action you can see the manifestations of God's Attributes. Yet in some things and some actions they are more apparent for our perception than others. By God breathing His spirit into us, we are endowed with the potential to perceive and manifest all of God's Attributes. Yet, we can manifest a few of them maybe, and perceive in creation only a few of them now, and through increasing our knowledge of God, start perceiving more and more. For instance, when we study the qualities of a single beam of light in a given room, we would know about all the other beams in the room. If we deny that one single photon from the sun is not coming from the sun, it is as if we are denying that all of the photons are from the sun.

Everything in creation manifests God's Attributes, and thus, everything is sacred in its creation (root of environmentalism in Islam). From this point of view, rendering anything worthless is like rendering its Maker worthless. The distinction to be aware of is that humans are sacred in their creation, yet the misuse of their freewill, choices, and false claims of denying God, may be worthless.

If someone deliberately chooses the wrong, tells a lie, or hurts others, then we cannot respect that choice, bad action, or thought. Yet we can and we should still respect his/her creation or being. When human beings misuse their freewill, the result of their choice is not perfect. Yet, if they repent, then this is, in a sense, correction bringing us back to perfection. The essence of the human being is always absolutely sacred and perfect.

If we spend all that is bestowed on us (our potential) for the purpose of our creation, all these qualities become like a map, explaining the reality of this universe. Our usage of the potential for the purpose it was given is praising/appreciating what has been given to us.

So the relation between the knowledge of God and praise of God lies here. If I know God, know His purpose in creation and me, and use what He has given to me as He intended them to be used, I am praising Him. This is active, physical praising. If I do not know why these qualities and this potential have been given to me, I cannot use it in the way it was meant, and cannot praise God. I would be insulting God if I wasted the qualities by using them in unrelated ways.

There is also verbal praising: praising the Giver with words after we experience the blessings. Divine Law removes the rust of nature. Divine Law is manifested in two ways. One is the way things have been set up in the universe. The other is the guidance conveyed through the scriptures. Rust of nature means understanding that things are happening, occurring, coming about naturally. Rust refers to covering up the truth in creation, cutting off the relationship of creation from its Creator. Thus, obeying God's commands in creation and in scriptures removes the rust of nature.

For example, we eat an orange. If while I am eating it, I get to know God's Attributes, I have praised God by obeying the purpose of the creation of the orange. But if I do not communicate with the orange in this way, and choose to block the Attributes of God (*kufr*: cover up), then I am saying that this orange is not a gift from God; it is there naturally, by itself. In this context, obeying the Divine Law means obeying the command of remembering God and observing the manifestations of His Attributes on the creation of the orange. Not wasting it while eating is also obeying the Divine Law prescribed for me in the scripture.

In the Afterlife, we will witness reality and there will be no way to cover up the truth or claim ownership. We will be conscious of our existence, and by default manifest God's Attributes (the ability to misuse our partial-freewill will not be functioning anymore). Thus our level of apprehension of beauty in this life is important, because we will enjoy the real beauty in the Afterlife in accordance with what we apprehended here.

We want to know God better, and enjoy the Afterlife. We must recognize and admit that it is not us who will gain paradise, but God will give us the apprehension/knowledge of God and paradise. For instance, if we think that the Creator is absolutely compassionate and merciful; in this understanding there is no room for hell. Hell is for those who deny the mercy of God. When we admit the mercy of God as absolute, we cannot say "I will be put in hell." God saying "I am as my servants think of me" (*Sahih al-Bukhari,* Tawhid, 15/35) means exactly this.

In other words, praise is the display of the attributes of perfection. A flower displays God's Attributes by default. But in human beings, if our freewill interferes, we might cover them up. So we need to just submit and let the Attributes of perfection manifest on us. In a sense, we have to choose to display what is already in us, like the flower. But we have been given an extra capacity to witness and confirm this display in other creatures as well.

Praising is fulfilling our purpose of creation by using the Attributes for the purpose they were given to us and by verbally praising the One who gave them. For example, my eyes are given to me to witness God's manifestations in creation in order to increase my knowledge of God. If I use my eyes like a rabbit, only to look for food, etc., then I am not giving due thanks for my eyes. Using our potentials for their intended purpose has to be conscious. This is the *fitri*, natural way of praising the Bestower or the active praise as opposed to verbal praise. (*Fitrah* means what has been purposefully given to us and how we were created, given attributes or potentialities, and our natural tendencies.)

Man is a summary of the universe in both spirit and body. Human beings are a place of manifestations of God's Attributes. Man is in the center like a prism that receives and refracts the light into its different colors. He is in the center of the world of the unseen and the world of the seen (*alam-ul-ghayb* and *alam-us-shahadah*).

World of the Unseen (Alam-ul-Ghayb)	→	Human	→	Observable World (Alam-us-Shahadah)

If we look at a man, we can deduce what the World of the unseen has. Sufi scholars tried to understand why humans were chosen as the representatives of God on earth, receiving commands from God and at the same time acting on earth as if they were the real owners—using things, being in charge, trying to understand and make sense of them in order to know the World of the Unseen, and represent it in this world. Human beings reflect God's Attributes of Perfection (since Adam, peace be upon him, was taught the names of creatures on the earth) and were given scales/gauges as a tool to measure, the quality of the Attributes but not the quantity. For instance, we have been given the ability to gauge compassion, ability to understand, measure what God's compassion is. We have been given limited knowledge so that we can comprehend what it means for God to be the All-Knower. Yet thinking that His knowledge is the ocean and ours is a drop from the ocean is wrong. This would wrongfully mean that we are part of God (and even part of Divine is Divine; hence this would be saying we are God). Ours is not a drop from the ocean. Ours is a measurement which measures the quality of water, rather than of the same kind of water.

We are given the capacity to appreciate, understand God's Attributes, but being able to appreciate is completely different than owning even a little piece of God's Knowledge. Our knowledge is not of the same type or quality as God's. If we say we have small pieces of God's Attributes, we are claiming to be small Gods, because small pieces of absolute are still absolute. Infinity divided by million is infinity. God blowing into us from His spirit must be understood in the same way. God reflected in man's being, the capacity to understand Him. Each fraction of my being demonstrates God's Absoluteness. We are from God but we are not a small piece of God. We are not of the same nature.

When I am acting compassionately, I am not representing God's compassion, but displaying that my Creator is the Compassionate One. We do not own anything, but we pretend that we own things. We must use our sense of ownership, the scale/gauge, as a measurement to understand God's ownership. What does God own? My ownership of a thing (trusteeship) is not of the same kind of God's ownership. Once we start to use this scale to understand God, we realize we do not own things. The first step is to feel like you own it.

Then you use the scale to understand what I own and what God's ownership means. The third is to extend this example, scale to all other feelings and qualities that I have been given as scales.

As a cognitive tool each of the senses, qualities are given to us. When we manifest His Attributes, we display that our Creator is compassionate. No one can claim the ownership of his/her attributes. Yet, in this world we have the option to not reflect them or claim ownership through our freewill, and exclaim "I am smart, I am tidy." The gist of praise of God is to employ the senses, qualities endowed on us by God, in measuring the Absolute Attributes of God that are manifested in the creation.

Renewing our Faith

An Exegesis of the Prophetic Saying:
"Renew your belief with 'There is no deity but God.'"

I s belief a fixed or a changeable phenomenon (whether or not it can increase or decrease)? Another related question, to which most scholars gave a positive answer, is whether belief is renewable. Since we are created with forgetful/neglectful natures, we forget or neglect our belief, so we need to renew/reconfirm it. But why would we need to reconfirm our belief once we have already affirmed our belief in God?

The primary reason why we are encouraged to renew our faith is simply because creation is continuously being renewed. Creation points us to the Creator, and we acquire belief through witnessing the manifestations of God's Attributes in the creation. Hence, as the universe changes, we need to reconfirm our belief in the Creator of that universe.

"Practice" does not only involve performing prescribed rituals. We have to also "practice believing." Belief is not static, but alive and dynamic. Belief is not a status that we obtain, such as identifying ourselves as a Muslim and thinking our duty is finished. Belief is not obtaining an identity card; belief lives with us and changes from minute to minute, hour to hour. God prescribed guiding rules that organize human relationships; plus another way of putting one's belief into practice is renewing our belief through the signs we observe in the universe.

Our duty is to reflect on the creation and to acknowledge the real source of everything. Human beings constantly undergo change. In every instance we need to establish the right relationship with God.

To see the manifestations of God's Attributes is the goal of our *iman* education. But this is not enough for a human being. We are created to have a relationship with the universe as well. While we have contact with the universe, we encounter manifestations of God's Attributes. The universe may not be according to our wishes all the time, so we need to interpret things and events that we encounter as manifestations of God's Attributes of Perfection. We are not tested only once, but in every event we encounter, we are being educated and tested. In institutionalized religion, you become a member of an institution, you pay for membership, you join the congregation, and this is it. Your closeness with God is not related to your active relationship with the universe. You get advice from the clergy, but in Islam there is no clergy. So we are responsible for our own beliefs; we are on our own. So we cannot just say I am a Muslim, I am a member of a mosque, and I come to Friday Prayer and so I am done. Religion is not an institution. Islam is submission; submission is a process; it is our relationship with our Creator.

Belief is not a claim, but a dynamic phenomenon. The most important aspect of Islam is the absence of institutions. From one aspect, the lack of institutions gives the believer freedom, yet from another aspect it gives greater responsibility since believers have a personal relationship with their Creator without an intermediary. Believing in your Creator is important, not the "God of your religion." My Creator creates the sun for me. This is a complete change in point of view. When you confirm that God is your Creator, then this is your definition of who you are: "I am a created being, a servant of God," and your life changes. Our faith must not only be strengthened when we go to the mosque. The entire universe is the house of God, and everything is prostrating to God. Our faith can only be strengthened when we contemplate on the signs/*ayah*s in the scriptures and the creation.

The universe is changing, so God's Attributes that I am supposed to witness are renewing as well. One second it is rainy, the next it becomes too sunny. Day and night change. Everything is constantly created anew. The same is true for human relations—each social event (say someone hurts you or someone pampers you) is a new opportunity for spiritual training. So in all our interactions (with other people, events, universe), there must be *la ilaha illallah* (there is no deity in creation, but God). Our relationship with the universe is the litmus test. Will I try to impose my expectations/desires onto the universe (which is impossible to accomplish and leads to stress/sorrow), or will I acknowledge that it is God who is organizing everything? No one says, "I will create the universe," but we struggle to accept that events do not go as we want. I do not want it to rain (hence its Creator), so I am protesting the rain as if it is in my hands.

The first thing we will be asked when we die is: *Man Rabbuk* (Who is your Lord/Sustainer/Caretaker/Educator)? The question is not only, "Who created you?" We need to recognize that God is the Creator, but that is only the beginning. We need to also confirm that in every instant of our lives God is our Sustainer, our Caretaker. As human beings and as *khalif* representing God on earth, we have been given the potential to manifest all of God's Attributes. We are the vicegerents or stewards of God on earth, because we can act here on behalf of God. All the abilities I have are from God, so I am acting in this world on behalf of God, in His name. This is why we are expected to act in accordance with the Attributes of God. For example, God is forgiving, merciful and just, so I cannot act without wisdom, justice, and mercy. This is my duty as God's vicegerent. We must try our best to choose the right thing, to reflect God's Attributes, as a creature of God. However, we have been given the freedom to choose not to reflect these Attributes. We have to be very careful not to choose against God's gifts to us—we should not be unjust, merciless, and foolish.

The other aspect of our stewardship is our relationship with the rest of the creation. When we interfere with the universe, we have to interfere in the name of God, not in the name of our desires. This is where the quarrel starts. I may appropriate God's Attributes to myself, forget that I am being created, not heed His guidance, and choose as I want (submit to God's Will vs. submit to my ego). If I forget I am here to act in the name of God, I start acting according to my own whims. We have to implement God's guidance into our life by using our freewill correctly. This is a personal responsibility. This is why there is no clergy in Islam. No one else can do it apart from me. The rules of the Qur'an are waiting to be implemented by human beings in their personal lives by themselves. This is why belief in God is a personal choice and a personal matter. Indeed we live in a society and have relationships, but we are personally responsible for our choices. If my friend is a *wali*, a friend of God, that does not save me. If somebody cannot give the *Rububiyyah* to God (admit that God is the Sustainer) in his own life, he cannot do it in his family, city, or country. This means acknowledging that God is the Creator and choosing to submit our freewill according to His will. Having a personal relationship with God is beautiful and safe. It is to know that you do not worship your own desires, nor can anyone bully you. Death is nothing to fear for such a believer. Even if we hear that doomsday is here, we say "my Most Compassionate Sustainer is operating it all," so we are relaxed. The key to inner peace is in this realization: "It is the All-Wise and the Most-Merciful One who is administering my life, not me!"

This is why the main question is Who is your *Rab*/Sustainer/Administrator? Not who created you? We need to realize that our belief is dynamic and needs to be continuously renewed.

We might talk of being a submitter to God at three interrelated levels. Practice of rituals (*ibadah*), practice of *shariah* (Divine laws/guidance) at the societal level, and the personal practice of one's belief, which is the core of everything. Living our belief entails living as the worshipper of God only. It is a personal conviction. To become part of the *ummah* (religious community), you need to submit yourself to God, not commit yourself to the *ummah*. For example, if you are going to college, and if you do not study well, you will be expelled from school. Even if you want to identify yourself with Purdue University and you wear a Purdue t-shirt, this does not make you a student there. The point of you being a part of the university is for you to learn and receive training. If you are not committed to your education, then there is no meaning for you to be part of the community anyways.

Claiming that I am a monotheist, there is only one God, is a necessary but not a sufficient enough step. A person might ask, "Yes, creation witnesses that there is only one God, but when it comes to my life, decisions I make about my life, in how I interact with others, who is going to decide? Is it me or the Creator? Will I submit to His guidance or act according to my desires?" Claiming to be a monotheist does not solve the problem. Usually if someone claims to be an atheist, it means "I could not find any way to submit; I am not ready to look for it at all." But if someone claims to be an agnostic, it means, "I know there is a God, but I do not want to submit to Him."

Being a servant of God is beautiful; it means you are free from all other thousands of servitudes. It means: relax! If you really believe in God, everything is guaranteed as He wills. And the good news is that the One who is in charge is the Most-Compassionate and the All-Wise...

Disbelief and Satan's Whisperings

S atan has no power over us, and this means that he does not have any real evidence to convince us that God does not exist. He just whispers an idea that does not have any substantial reason. For instance, no one can really prove that there is no God since everything points to God's existence. Everything in a building says that there is a builder. Doubt, imagination, insecurity, or fear is not evidence to follow Satan. These feelings are in fact given to us to urge us to investigate God. In the absence of these feelings, we would have no impulse to search for the truth. Belief in the existence of God starts with curiosity and the resulting search for a satisfactory answer.

Kafir (a person who denies God by covering up the truth) exists, but *kufr* (denial of the truth) does not have an external existence. It is only the absence of something (not reflecting God's Attributes from our mirror). The absence of one is zero, and zero does not have a reality/existence. It is only the absence of something. We must not believe in dogmas, because only disbelief is dogma (since it cannot bring any evidence). If I consider myself a Muslim and believe in the existence of the Hereafter, these are dogmas only if I do not bring any evidence. With the evidence of the universe, it is clear that there is a Creator. Thus, we must not present our belief in the form of dogma. Instead we must see that everything is planned. If there was any single cell or atom in the universe that did not have an Omniscient and Omnipotent Creator, then disbelief in the Orderer of the universe/God would be justified.

God is the Most-Merciful and does not leave us without guidance to figure out what is going on. He brings evidence and guidelines for us. The verse, *"We have not sent you (O Muhammad) but as an unequalled mercy for all the worlds"* (al-Anbiya 21:107) means that you personally were sent to be a guide, and this is in itself a mercy. Creation is already evidence, but as a bonus, the Messengers are sent. In a way this saying also tells the Prophet: "Your mission must be in the form of mercy; be compassionate." We may not be ready to submit to the truth, but we can admit the presence of an Orderer, a Creator.

Significance of *Halal* and *Haram*

Many Muslims understand Islam mostly in terms of *halal* (permissions) and *haram* (prohibitions), excessively and/ or exclusively emphasizing the do's and don'ts. These concepts do exist in Islam and circle the frontiers of where a believer should or should not be. However, the real question is: Once we choose to be inside this circle and know the boundaries, what are we going to do inside? For instance, we know drinking alcohol is *haram* (forbidden) and water is *halal*. But how should our relationship with water be so that we are an *abd* (servant of God)? How can we have a worshipper's relationship with the world since the Qur'an persistently reminds us that everything is a sign? Many people may not drink alcohol because they dislike it; so what is the difference between the one who is seeking to be a worshipper and an unbeliever, who also avoids alcohol?

When *hadith* or the Qur'an says "act in the name of God (*bismillah*)," it does not only mean "say" *bismillah*. Saying it is meant to remind us of something else. As a worshipper, we are to do the *halal* in the name of God, and *bismillah* is only the remembrance (*thikr*) or the reminder. *Thikr* is as important as Prayer (*salat*), because it is what makes the prayer meaningful. You may perform an entire *salat* without thinking of God once, whereas *dhikr* (remembrance) is the essence of worship. Thus, saying *bismillah* is only the beginning of a lifelong education (*tarbiyah*). This is why the Companions of Prophet Muhammad, peace and blessings be upon him, did not just learn the list of what is *halal* and what is *haram*; this would not have taken 23 years to learn! Moreover, at the beginning of the revelation of the Qur'an, there was not a concept of *halal* and *haram* yet. These concepts came after *iman* was established in their hearts, and they have received the *tarbiyah* of the Qur'an. Because when one has the essence, *amal* (deeds) are like the skin of the fruit. The skin is needed to protect and nourish the fruit so it can grow. The skin is therefore crucial for preserving the core.

If we do not have the boundaries, or the setting in which the core can grow, we will not know how to practice submission and *tawhid*. Thus deeds, do's and don'ts, are facilitating worship, but the goal is *ibadatullah* (worship of God) not the *amal* on its own. To do everything in the name of God is *ibadah* (worship). Hence, we need to learn more than just memorizing the do's and don'ts. For instance, if I fast during Ramadan and do not feel anything other than hunger, would this really be fasting? Whereas the *amal* is the psychical form of expressing the belief, the *niyah* (intention) is very important in order to be actually worshipping. If someone comes and starts imitating the *salat* (prescribed Prayers) without intending to do it in the name of God, it would not be considered *salat*. The relationship between the outer form of deeds and the inner dimensions resembles the relationship of the spirit (*ruh*) and the body. The *ruh* cannot experience anything without the body. Yet, the body would be dead without the *ruh*, so they are both important to coexist. In a *hadith qudsi*, Prophet Muhammad, peace and blessings be upon him, related God's message as:

> A servant [of Allah] committed a sin and said: O Allah, forgive me my sin. And He (glorified and exalted be He) said: My servant has committed a sin and has known that he has a Lord who forgives sins and punishes for them. Then he sinned again and said: O Lord, forgive me my sin. And He (glorified and exalted be He) said: My servant has committed a sin and has known that he has a Lord who forgives sins and punishes for them. Then he sinned again and said: O Lord, forgive me my sin. And He (glorified and exalted be He) said: My servant has committed a sin and has known that he has a Lord who forgives sins

and punishes for sins. Do what you wish, for I have forgiven
you. (*Sahih al-Bukhari,* Tawhid, 15).

This *hadith* does not imply we can sin as we like and God will
forgive us no matter what. The condition for forgiveness is that every
time we sin, we sincerely repent and come back asking for forgiveness from God. The essential point here is that asking for forgiveness
implies the acknowledgment of having a Lord; accepting His Lord-
ship and Mercy and asking for forgiveness.

The greatest sin, and the only one that will not be forgiven, is
shirk (associating partners with God = violating *tawhid*). It is on the
level of belief and disbelief and not the less significant *halal* and *haram*
level. Hence, we should focus on understanding *shirk* so we do not
commit it, because according to this *hadith* we will be forgiven as long
as we return to God and do not violate *tawhid*. *Tawhid* is so important
that the entire Qur'an is about it. The fact that the Qur'an was revealed
gradually over 23 years is noteworthy. The Companions of the Prophet were gradually educated by the Qur'an to live by *tawhid*. Yet, we
have the entire Qur'an as a book now, so we mistakenly think that
'saying' the declaration of faith (*shahadah*) makes us a *muslim*/submit-
ter. However, what will save us is our understanding of God's grace
and living by *tawhid* and *ikhlas* (sincerity). The goal is not total self-pu-
rification, and we can never be sure that we have no sins. The goal is
to continuously recognize our *ubudiyyah* (our being created). The attitude, "I have no sins so you have to put me in Heaven now," contradicts the spirit of *tawhid*. The point is to know our position before the
mercy of God. In a *hadith qudsi*, Prophet Muhammad, peace and blessings be upon him, relates God's message as:

O son of Adam, so long as you call upon Me and ask of Me, I
shall forgive you for what you have done, and I shall not mind.
O son of Adam, were your sins to reach the clouds of the sky
and were you then to ask forgiveness of Me, I would forgive
you. O son of Adam, were you to come to Me with sins nearly
as great as the earth and were you then to face Me, ascribing

no partner to Me, I would bring you forgiveness nearly as great as it. (*Sunan at-Tirmidhi*, Da'awat, 106).

This *hadith qudsi*, like the previous one, warns us not to over-emphasize sin and *halal/haram* at the expense of *iman*, but to focus on *tawhid* and *ikhlas* (sincerity). These sacred sayings instruct us to make sure we are not committing *shirk*. When we focus on *halal* and *haram*, we tend to say "I am on the *halal* side so I am fine/safe." This attitude itself is on the path of *shirk* because it assumes that it is me who is doing the *halal*, not seeing it as God's grace. Thus it is not humble, and it can easily lead to *shirk*. The goal is to close all the ways that might lead to *shirk*. Someone who really knows God and the true meaning of unifying God/*tawhid* in daily life is less likely to commit *shirk*. This requires practicing our faith; putting it in practice in our daily life. We tend to forget about our purpose of creation, which is to worship our Creator, to know ourselves and our purpose in life and relation with God. It is not about do's and don'ts, which may be called the mechanics of religion.

The mechanics are there to help us with the essentials (i.e. *iman*). When we falsely think we are the one performing things, we feel better about our ego/*nafs*. For example, we have lost if we say "I am sincere," by attributing our accomplishments to ourselves. *Ikhlas* is to know that everything is from God and nothing is from us. Understanding this is a lifetime process. We will experience and recognize it at different levels through different phases of our life. This is why the Qur'an descended over 23 years. It is not a set amount of knowledge or information that we memorize or can be spoon fed. We ought to strive to be educated and transformed by its guidance.

The aforementioned *hadith qudsi* tell us not to focus on sin. It is one of Satan's tricks to render us hopeless by whispering "you sinned so much, your prayer is not worth anything." Losing hope of God's mercy is sign of unbelief. When we concentrate on deeds/*amal*, we can easily lose hope, because we can never be sure our deeds are good enough. The focus should always be on asking God to make our deeds acceptable by praying: "God, my intention was to worship you, so please purify my intention and accept my deeds." Doing the best action, etc. is not the point. The point is to return to Him and ask from Him, because acknowledging His mercy is important. The *salat* is only a reminder of our state of worship. If our *salat* is not increasing our *iman* in God, it means we do not have the right attitude and the right understanding of *ibadah* (worship).

Prayer

Call upon your Lord (O humankind) with humility and in the secrecy of your hearts... (al-A'raf 7:55)

Remember and mention your Lord within yourself (in the depths of your heart), most humbly and in awe, not loud of voice, at morning and evening. And do not be among the neglectful. (al-A'raf 7:205)

What is a prayer? It is supplication; dialogue between a person and the Diving Being; demonstration of one's reliance; communication through which we gain confidence and clarity in our being and our Creator. But first and foremost, it is an act of submission. When we pray, we acknowledge that there is a Divine Being who has power and control and we need Him.

When we say prayer, the first thing that comes to our mind is a person supplicating to God through words. However, when we take a holistic perspective on prayer, we realize that everything in creation is in a state of prayer, in one form or another. For instance, a baby, is in a state of prayer. His existence is a sort of prayer, admitting that he cannot do anything and is asking others to do things for him. We can generalize this example to all beings. Nothing can sustain its existence on its own. So everything is, subconsciously or consciously, asking the One to sustain their existence. In this sense, the innate disposition of everything is prayer; recognizing and accepting of their reality, and confessing their imperfection and need.

If prayer is not seen in this way, it becomes an expectation for magic. We pray to have a car and wait to see a car fall out of thin air. The conventional understanding of prayer is that when you lose your job, you ask for a job. To the contrary, we are to pray consciously as human beings using our freewill. The real prayer is recognizing who we are, what the universe is, whom we are addressing in our prayers.

Let's take a closer look at the Lord's Prayer: Thine is the Kingdom (*lahul mulku*) and the power (*lahul hawlu*) and the glory (*hamdu*) forever (*abadan*). This statement carries the gist of prayer. It is not asking for anything directly. We are communicating with the Creator, and telling Him "Yours is the kingdom and power and glory." Since He already knows who He is, why do we say this? In order to know whom we are communicating with, we state these qualities for ourselves, not for Him. Therefore, stating who the addressee is and knowing who we are is real supplication. Thus, the aim of prayer is to remind ourselves of our reality —that we are a created being who is infinitely dependent on our Creator who is All-Powerful, All-Knowing, and All-Wise. When a rain drop is falling, it has no choice but to obey the laws of God (i.e. gravity). It is created and dropped by Him, in His Universe. When we eat or walk, we are praying to God to be able to eat and walk by obeying His laws (i.e. eating, digestion, having to sleep, having to blink, etc.). Seen this way, we could categorize prayer into three groups:

1. Praying through latent ability; e.g. seeds and grains.
2. Praying through innate need; e.g. causes seeking effects.
3. Prayers of conscious beings:
   a. By action; e.g. sowing a seed.
   b. By word.

First, everything prays to its Creator with its latent ability, e.g.seeds and grains: The gathering together of causes is a prayer for the creation of the effect. The apple seed is in prayer to become an apple tree. Its innate and latent ability shows that it wants to be an apple tree; it is made to be an apple tree. How do we understand that they are praying? Just by looking at the seed we see that they do not have any power, knowledge, or capacity to grow the apple tree. Its prayer is answered when the Creator gives it the apple tree. From one aspect, they demonstrate that they cannot realize their potentials on their own. What we see in the universe is but a prayer to God.

Second, all living creatures pray to God through their innate need to give them the things they need and desire, which are beyond their power and will: Those things that are causes seek the effects from God. Every plant, as it demonstrates its need, is praying to give its final intended fruit. Our ears need to hear, our stomachs need food. This need is a prayer in itself. If we disassociate this need from our relation/communication with our Creator, then this need does not become a form of prayer. If we think we are self-sufficient, we are cutting off our praying relationship with our Creator. But apart from human beings, all creatures by default admit their dependency on God. Through their need they pray: "I cannot provide it; some other source must provide it for me." When we are supplicating with our tongue, all we are doing is reaffirming/joining the universal supplication of all creatures, as well as body, senses, intellect, etc.

The first two types of prayer, through latent ability and innate need, are always answered. For instance, we are hungry and the food is already created; we need to walk and we are given the ability to walk, etc. However, as conscious beings, we are responsible for using our conscience and freewill to do the third type of prayer.

Third, the prayer of conscious beings arising from need: Prayer is the most sacred action of human beings. What we are actually doing is joining creation and following the example of their prayer. As conscious beings, we pray through action and through words.

The prayer of conscious beings through action: For example, plowing is a prayer by action. It is not seeking the sustenance from the earth. Rather, the earth is a door to a treasury of mercy, and the plow knocks on the earth: the door to Divine Mercy. Whether or not the farmer accepts that it is not earth but God who gives the products, this prayer is still answered. So if he thinks it is coming from nature, this conscious choice is wrong, but the action of plowing is a type of prayer that is rewarded. It is in the laws of creation that if we sow a seed, it sprouts. We do not have to be a believer for the seed to sprout. So this type of prayer is also always accepted.

Human beings also make prayers at times of desperate need, or completely conformable with innate need, or made with the tongue of a sincere heart. This prayer is virtually always acceptable. The greater part of human progress and most scientific discoveries are the result of this sort of prayer.

And finally, the prayer of conscious beings through words: After we sow the seed (prayer by action), we pray to God with words to create tomatoes for us; after we study hard (prayer by action), we ask God to get a good grade; after we go to the doctor and take our medication (prayer by action), we ask God to heal us; after we exert all effort to behave kindly towards our friend (by action), we ask God to amend our relationship, etc.

Prayer is the spirit of worship and the result of sincere belief. Through prayer, the worshipper proclaims his or her own impotence and poverty. Praying is an acknowledgment that there is a Divine Being who rules the whole universe, and that He hears all the voices of all beings, including ours.

There is a wise saying that goes, "If He did not will to give, He would not give the desire to want." God responds to our prayers according to His wisdom; e.g. the doctor listens to the sick person's sighs and moans; he hears and responds to them. The sweetest result of prayer is that when it is offered, there is someone who takes pity and whose hand of power reaches everything. He is not alone in this great hostel of the world. The benefits of prayer also include eternal life. If the worldly aims are not obtained, it may not be said, "The prayer was not accepted." It should rather be said, "The time of the prayer has still not ended." As prayer strengthens the inclination to do good, repentance and the seeking of forgiveness cut the inclination to do evil, putting an end to its transgressions.

God says in the Qur'an, *"... Pray to me and I will answer you..."* (al-Mumin 40:60). Yet sometimes we think our prayers are not answered. Prayers are answered in three forms: a) what we asked for is granted as is, b) something that is better than what we asked for is granted, c) the response is deferred to the afterlife. When we go to the doctor and ask for medicine A, the doctor would give it to us if it is what we need. Or he would give us medicine B saying that either medicine A would actually make our illness worse or simply that medicine B would help us heal better and faster. Alternatively, the doctor may say, the best cure for your case is to wait it out... This analogy helps us to contemplate on our prayers and God's response to our prayers. Sometimes we ask for things, but we do not possess knowledge of the future. What we are asking for may in fact be terrible for us. So it is wise to always say: "O God, I am asking for such and such but you know best, please give it to me if it is *khayr*/good for me..."

Fasting[22]

The month of Ramadan (is the month) in which the Qur'an was sent down as guidance for people, and as clear truths of the guidance and the Criterion (between truth and falsehood). Therefore, whoever of you is present this month must fast it...
(al-Baqarah 2:185)

Fasting is a type of worship that is shared among the three Abrahamic traditions, though in unique forms. God prescribes healthy adult believers to fast from sunrise to sunset during the month of Ramadan, which is the ninth month in the lunar calendar. Indeed, we are encouraged to fast throughout the year, and some believers follow the tradition of Prophet Muhammad, peace and blessings be upon him, to fast Mondays and Thursdays. One of the significances of the month of Ramadan is the fact that the Qur'an was first revealed in this month.

Fasting means not eating or drinking; no water, no smoking, no gum. Yet, it also entails much more than that. All other faculties fast as well. For instance, our tongue fasts by not getting angry, lying, breaking someone's heart, being mean, etc. Our eyes fast by not looking at unlawful things. Our entire body fasts by using it in acts that would please God, like helping others. Moreover, fasting is to be accompanied by heightened spirituality; trying to get closer to God, increasing our awareness that He is the sole Creator and Sustainer of everything. The Ramadan fast is an intensive course of focusing on

---

[22] In preparing this section, I have benefitted from Nursi's "Treatise on Ramadan" (Twenty-Ninth Letter). I also thank Dr. İsra Yazıcıoğlu for sharing her reflections on this chapter.

worship, contemplation, and social service, such as helping the needy and feeding the poor.

Why was fasting prescribed? What is the wisdom in it? For one, it helps us to see the bigger picture, to see order, the Orderer, and Wisdom and Mercy in everything through contemplation. The Creator knows us better than us. Religion is His guidance and our manual. So we choose to follow this guidance to fulfill the purpose of our creation and to find inner peace. It is healthy for our body and soul, and it disciplines our ego. It helps us to realize our weakness and neediness, which makes us more humble and modest. Fasting teaches us to be more thankful for all blessings. We need to understand hunger and help others. Experience equals confirmation.

If a person goes to a friend's house, the feast might be ready, but the guest won't start eating until his host invites him. Why does he wait? Out of respect and to show that he acknowledges and cares for his host. During the month of Ramadan, the month of fasting, it's very much like that: We wait all day, from sunrise to sunset, for our Divine Host to invite us to eat and drink when the call to prayer is recited.

This is an extraordinary experience. Although it's not easy to fast, when it's time to break the fast at sunset, there is that wonderful feeling of belonging, of being the guest of the Divine, the guest of the compassionate Creator and Provider. And we rejoice not only at satisfying our hunger but more so at being the guest of the Lord.

Ramadan is a time to refresh the way we look at the world. It makes us reflect on the "simple" things that are in fact amazing. Even a cup of tea is not as cheap as it seems to be. For a tea leaf to grow, the existence of the whole universe is required: the sun, the rotation of the earth, the rain, soil, bacteria, and so on. Have you ever tried to count the kinds of fruits, vegetables, plants that "come out" of the soil? Is it a simple process?

The Creator has made the whole world like a feast, showing His generosity and compassion. Yet, in daily life we often forget to respond appropriately to these glorious acts of the Creator. And in order to be thankful to God we need to remember that we are given all these gifts, but we also need to recognize the value of the gifts. We quite often underestimate the value of a glass of water or a piece of bread until we give up the daytime meals and snacks in the month of Ramadan. This makes fasting during Ramadan a powerful means of recovering our gratitude to our Merciful Sustainer. When we fast, we are hungry and we appreciate the value of food; we realize what a precious gift it is and we are filled with gratitude. This makes us reflect on the countless gifts and blessings that we have been given; not only food and drink, but also health, sight, friendship, air, water, etc. Everything is valuable; everything is a blessing.

Fasting allows us to become more conscious of the compassionate sustainer of the world, and so we turn to our Lord to acknowledge our gratitude. We remember once more that we are guests of God on earth. In Ramadan, we become like an assembly of guests waiting for the invitation of our host to start enjoying the feast. We respectfully wait in front of the dinner table for the Glorious Host's invitation to start eating. The fast of Ramadan helps us remember that we are being taken care of with compassion and generosity.

Everything becomes a sign that speaks of God's generosity and compassion. Food becomes a token of love, a sign of divine favor; a sign that turns our attention from the food itself to the Bestower of the food. We also understand that hunger has not been given to us only to fill our stomachs and derive temporary pleasure from it, but to make that pleasure itself a sign, a means to recognize the giver of the pleasure and turn to Him. And when the food is perceived as a Divine favor, the pleasure it gives is far greater than the pleasure obtained from its perishable matter. It gives a lasting delight: the pleasure of feeling in the presence of God's everlasting compassion and love. That is why every time we break the fast, we experience the good news of everlasting pleasure and we rejoice. Every evening in the month of fasting is a feast. And at the end of the month, the whole community celebrates the feast of the breaking of the fast.

Like Ramadan, *Eid* or feasting is centered on worship rather than food. However, food is always present during *Eid* too, because in

Islam, everything in the world is sacred; every event is a sign pointing to its Maker. The feast is celebrated with communal prayers and
glorification of God that lasts three days. People visit each other and
offer presents to each other to express their gratitude to God.

Feasting is basically rejoicing at being the honored guest of the
compassionate Creator, the host. We rejoice at God's love and care
for us as His guests here on earth. Fasting during Ramadan is the
opportunity to remember God's loving presence and to hold our
hearts open to receive His compassionate guidance and help.

Technically speaking, the fast of Ramadan is one of the pillars of
Islam. Like other pillars of Islam, it has personal, social and ethical
implications. It refreshes our relationship to our Merciful Creator as
well as our relations with other human beings. It is basically a month
of thanksgiving at various personal and social levels. When we fast,
we realize how weak we are; how fragile the human body is; how
dependent we are on so many things we take for granted. It's a situation that makes us wonder who we really are. Our needs are countless, but usually we are not even aware of them because we take them
for granted. The more we realize how needy we are, the more we feel
that we are bombarded with blessings, and our whole being is filled
with gratitude for the compassionate Creator, and when we surrender to this reality, we say, "Praise be to God, Lord of all the Worlds,"
which means the Lord of all gifts, the Lord of everything. And praising the merciful Creator is the essence of worship.

Therefore, fasting reminds us of our needs, and our needs are the
means to taste all gifts and enjoy them. Without hunger, food would
not provide pleasure. Our needs are also the means to feel empathy
for the needy; through our needs we communicate with the rest of
the world in the name of God, the provider of all. This makes us realize that we are not alien to other people or to other beings. That is
why we rejoice at the month of Ramadan even if our stomachs cry
out. And maybe that's why it is said that fasting brings about spiritual fulfillment and that in the month of fasting, rewards are multiplied
manifold. Ramadan is also often called the month of blessings.

When we empathize with others, and feel that we are not alien to them, then we can share everything with everybody because we are not anxious about providing for our needs. The Merciful Creator has already taken care of them. We are liberated from the illusory world of the ego that thinks that it provides for itself. Giving and sharing with others does not feel like a sacrifice anymore because nothing is ours anyway; everything is given to us. Sharing with others is an opportunity for us to remember and affirm this reality. Sharing becomes a source of joy, a source of realizing our position as honored guests of our Lord.

When we fast with this awareness, we remember the true owner of blessings and lovable things. Food becomes not mere perishable food, but a gift from God that is to be eaten in the name of God. We then love food in the name of its Maker who made it lovable and offered it to us as a gift of love and friendship. So Ramadan is a month of worship, a time to draw closer to God. It is a special time God chooses to open His extra doors of mercy.

What are the wisdoms of the Ramadan fast? The fast of Ramadan is one of the pillars of Islam. Like others pillars of Islam, it is a multifaceted act, with profound implications for all aspects of our lives, personal, social and ethical. It rejuvenates our relationship to our Merciful Creator, as well as our relations with other human beings. It helps us to be witnesses to God's glory, be mindful of and thankful for bounties of God, as well as to discipline our ego. In what follows, we will explore some of these aspects of Ramadan fast.

Ramadan fast is a witness to Our Sustainer. It is a time to refresh the way we view the world. It makes us reflect on the "simple" things that are in fact awesome. Even an apple is not as cheap as we regard it to be. For the growth of a single apple, the existence of whole universe is required: sun, the ordered rotation of earth, rain, soil, bacteria and so on. Indeed, Glorious Creator has made the whole world like a feast table; showing His perfect art, generosity and mercy. Yet, in daily life we often forget to respond appropriately to these glorious acts of the Creator.

It is in Ramadan that we wake up to a greater consciousness of this merciful and magnificent sustaining of the world. And, we turn all together, as a unified body of hundreds of millions—even more—believers around the globe, to acknowledge our gratitude to our Lord. We remember once more that we are guests of God on earth, and we show a palpable sign of this by actually participating in the fast of Ramadan. Indeed, in Ramadan, we become like a great assembly of royal guests waiting the command of their host in the dining hall to start enjoying the royal feast. All the Muslims around the globe become one united body, respectfully waiting in front of the dinner tables, for the Glorious Host's invitation to start eating. The fast of Ramadan helps us to remember our relationship to the Glorious Creator, as servants in awe and with gratitude.

Ramadan fast enhances our gratitude to our Creator. More specifically, Ramadan is a time to recover our gratitude to God. If a dear friend of yours sent you precious gifts in the mail, would you contend by thanking the mailperson? Would it be fair for you to forget to thank the sender, while thanking and tipping the deliverer? Yet, we frequently behave like this, when we receive gifts from God, such as life, health, food, drink or love, we contend ourselves by thanking only (or mainly) the 'deliverers' of these gifts—parents, friends, or nature, forgetting the Real Giver of these gifts. We may buy some bananas or a box of strawberries from the grocery store. As long as we pay several dollars for it, we think we really paid for these. While, in fact, we are only paying for the cultivation and transportation of these fruits. We are not paying for its amazing creation from a mixture of mud, or our capacity to taste, enjoy and digest these fruits. Do any of us, for instance, pay for the sun to shine or for the taste buds in our tongue to work?

Indeed, we need some boost in our recognition of the real Sender. One of the wisdoms in Ramadan fast is to get this boost. By being barred from eating till the time determined by the Creator (we may not start eating even a minute before the sunset call), we realize that what we thought as ours is not really ours. This discipline helps us to tell ourself: "Here it is, the vegetables I bought with my money and cooked with my own hands in my own oven heat. Yet, this food is really not mine, for I cannot eat it whenever I want. I have to wait for the permission of their Real Owner in the sunset." This concrete realization that all that we take for granted are gifts from God encourages us to be more thankful to Him. Nevertheless, while doing this we need not decrease our thanks to the 'deliverers' (so do not give up paying for the grocery bills!)

In order to be thankful to God we need not only remember that all are gifts from Him, but we also need to recognize the value of what is given. We quite often underestimate the value of a glass of water or a piece of bread until we give up the daytime meals and snacks in the month of Ramadan. Thus, Ramadan becomes a powerful way of recovering our gratitude to our Merciful Sustainer.

Ramadan fast is a means of getting to know who we are. God says in the Qur'an, *"Be not like those who are forgetful of God, and whom therefore [God] causes to forget themselves"* (al-Hashr 59:19). He reminds us of our reality:

> O humankind! You are all poor before God and in absolute need of Him, whereas He is the All-Wealthy and Self-Sufficient (absolutely independent of creation), the All-Praiseworthy (as your Lord, Who provides for you and all other beings, supplying all your needs. (Fatir 35:15)

Our ego wants to pretend as if it is independent of God; it does not want to admit its full dependence on its Creator, and wants to ignore the fact that it is a recipient and not the owner of the bounties of God. In short, we have a part in us that simply does not want to be grateful and humble before the Creator. Add economic affluence and worldly power to this innate inclination of our ego, we may easily end up with a life based on forgetfulness of God, living like a thief of God's bounties, devouring the bounties without acknowledging the Real Owner! The good news is that this ego is not what we are all about; it is just a part in us, it is not our real identity. The ego's innate duty is to encourage us to forget God, and our innate duty is to say "no" to it (i.e. to strengthen our muscles we have to lift weight). Ramadan fast is a time for us to do our job of honesty, when it palpably manifests that we are all needy recipients of God's sustenance. We realize in Ramadan more profoundly that we are neither self-sufficient nor immortal as our ego falsely claims. Our ego wants to overlook the fact that we are indeed weak, perishable mortals on earth. Our ego often wants to pretend that we are immortal, it wants to overlook the fact that we are only transient passengers on this world, destined for an eternal life in the Hereafter (and therefore need to prepare for it.) Fasting becomes a good discipline for our ego's illusions, by showing how our batteries fall low and our bodies become weak after hours of no ingestion. In Ramadan, the ego's tendency to play God like a Pharaoh vanishes and our human reality becomes manifest: We are all poor creatures before God, with perishable bodies, and we are better off by admitting this before our Creator.

Ramadan is also a time to draw closer to Our Creator, for it is a special time He chooses to open His extra doors of mercy. Moreover, Ramadan has social implications; it reminds us that an important component of being grateful for what God has given is to share it with our fellow human beings. Ramadan fast also helps spiritual growth by disciplining the "stomach," and enabling an environment in which we can listen to the message of the Qur'an more attentively.

Modest Dress and Etiquette (*Adab*)

One common question that Muslims are asked in the United States is why Muslim women cover themselves from head to toe. The reason behind this is actually similar to the reasons that a Catholic nun or an orthodox Jewish woman covers herself. In the Christian tradition, Mary the mother of Jesus is almost exclusively portrayed as wearing a head covering.

There are innumerable similarities between the three monotheistic traditions of Judaism, Christianity, and Islam. The central goal of the religious journey in these Abrahamic traditions is to acknowledge the Creator and to love Him by obeying His wise and compassionate guidance. A common area where almost all the doctrines of the three traditions overlap unquestionably is morality. Decency, chastity, modesty, righteousness, and purity are virtues that believers are encouraged to develop and required to struggle to achieve.

When people look at Muslim women who wear a headscarf, usually they only notice the headscarf as being different than Western style clothing. Many believers who wear a headscarf prefer to use the term 'modest dress' since it captures the essence of the practice. Modest dress is prescribed to both men and women in the Qur'an. The general guidelines include covering certain parts of the body, wearing loose and non-transparent clothing to conceal the silhouette, and to dress in such a way as to not draw attention to one's self. Men are advised to cover between the knees and the naval, whereas for women the only parts that can be revealed are face, hands, and feet. This difference is solely due to the physical nature and attractiveness of the female body and should not be misinterpreted as gender inequality.

Nevertheless, some people have a hard time grasping why the covering of hair is so important. Firstly, the hair is only one of the many parts that need to be covered. Secondly, if hair were not so attractive, women would not spend hours in front of the mirror or spend hundreds of dollars to make their hair pretty! However, the concept of covering in Islam is not restricted to only the headscarf, which would be undermining the meaning and effect of this practice. The underlying principle is to keep your beauty to yourself, your spouse, and those of the same sex, so you are not viewed as an "object." The ultimate goal of modest dress is to be modest in front of God and other human beings. Western feminists contend that one of the greatest problems of our age is the reduction of women to mere objects that are valued only by their physical beauty. The Muslim value of modest dress actually helps to combat this objectification of women. It is important to note that in Islam, physical beauty and marital relations are not viewed as a sin or something to be ashamed of. They are a gift of God, and we are to enjoy them within the limits prescribed by God.

In the Qur'an, God has commanded believing "men" and believing "women" to act in certain ways to avoid indecent interaction with the opposite sex, which bears great repercussions for individuals and society in this world and the Hereafter. Islam is a religion of prevention and protection, rather than a religion of punishment. All aspects of Islamic law aim to prevent sin in order to avoid punishment that would otherwise be necessary to ensure perfect justice. (It is also important to point out that in Islam, the concept of 'sin' is regarded as a transgression against one's self or a state of being away from God and acting contrary to our own nature). In other words, God knows His creatures and their weaknesses the best and puts guidelines to keep them from sinning because of His love and mercy for His creatures. Modest dress also has the same logic and nature. God has commanded it in the Qur'an, and Prophet Muhammad, peace and blessings be upon him, implemented it in his life and taught it to his followers for sound and compelling reasons.

The practice of wearing modest dress existed in various cultures and religions prior to the advent of Islam. Islam did not invent modest dress, but rather, adopted it from other traditions. Veiling (I use the term to refer to wearing a headscarf and not to veiling or covering the face as the term 'veil' may connote) was a common practice in Byzantine Empire during the Hellenistic era and also the Sassanid of Persia. The veil was a sign of respectability and high status and was used to distinguish nobles from the slaves and unchaste women who were not allowed to cover their heads. Subsequently, the practice was established in Judaic and Christian systems[23]. Arab societies adopted the veil from these cultures, and veiling gradually became a public practice even prior to the advent of Islam.

Judaic doctrines and traditions have emphasized the covering of hair and modest dress throughout history. Rabbinic law forbids the recitation of prayers in the presence of a bareheaded married woman, since it is considered nudity.[24] Jewish women in Europe wore headscarf until the end of nineteenth century when the pressures of a secular society triumphed over religion. Today, many Jewish women would cover their hair in Synagogues, yet only certain sects such as Hasidic Jews continue the practice in everyday life with wearing a wig.

The place of veiling in Christianity is as prevalent as in Judaism. The most obvious sign is the modest dress the nuns have been wearing for centuries. Veiling was part of the Christian tradition, not exclusively for nuns: *"And Rebekah* lifted up her eyes and when she saw Isaac... she took her *veil and covered herself"* (Genesis: 24:65). The Catholic Church had a canon up until 1950s requiring the women to cover their hair inside the church. Certain Christian denominations such as the Amish and the Mennonites still retain a head covering for the women.

Likewise, there is a strong connection between clothing, modesty, and morality in Islam. Thus, the concept of modesty extends beyond mere clothing and encompasses austere manners. This ideal

---

[23] Esposito 1995, p. 108.
[24] Muhammad 2003, p. 42.

code of conduct and modest dress are required from both men and women. There is strong emphasis on the protection of people's dignity in the Qur'an. (For instance, assaulting someone with words or slander is a grave transgression). One of the most compelling reasons for modest dress in the Qur'an is modesty and to protect women from harassment. It is not a sign of male superiority or of high status, as was the case in ancient societies.

First and foremost, it is essential to know that *"There is no compulsion in religion..."* (al-Baqarah 2:256). Faith is a personal matter between a believer and her Creator. Likewise, choosing to put one's faith into practice is a natural outcome of the believer's spiritual journey.

My personal division to start wearing the headscarf came after about two years of soul searching. Despite being raised in a Muslim family and a predominantly Muslim society, I was taken by the numerous positivist philosophies sweeping away young generations. I did have a vague belief in God that I never really thought about and confirmed in my heart and my mind. Hence, I did not really know what I believed in and why, which made it all the easier to drift away with currents of disbelief. I cannot thank God enough though for bringing certain seemingly "difficult" incidents to my life that forced me to question who I was and where I was going.

In retrospect, my decision to wear the headscarf for life came from a personal quest that can be recapped as follows. First, instead of shutting off the existential questions as I had been doing for years, I chose to try and find satisfying answers. Using the numerous faculties (like mind, heart, intellect, senses, etc.) that God has given me, I witnessed that there is no deity but God. I observed that God is the Creator of causes and their effects simultaneously. This confirmation compelled me to heed the message of God (scriptures) and to read it with an open mind and heart to confirm its truth. Once I confirmed that the Qur'an is indeed my Creator's message sent "to me personally" to inform me of my purpose of creation, then my worldview was transformed.

In a way, the Qur'an is like a manual. It is "my" manual, teaching me how to best use my faculties and my life. God is telling me why and how He creates me (what my reality is) and what sort of attitude and conduct is in harmony with my creation (my nature, *fitrah*). If I follow His recommendations, which are glad tidings for me (*bushra*), I will be at peace with myself and the universe. He also warns that when I do not follow the instructions in the manual, I may harm and even destroy myself, because I will be unhappy and live in a "hellish" state of mind and heart in this life and the Hereafter. Because we are given freewill, it is ultimately my choice to heed and follow this manual or not. And every believer can experience and attest to the truth of the message in her life (or not).

Analyzing the messages in the Qur'an from this paradigm, we may find endless wisdom and mercy in its recommendations. The following is a summary of the many wisdoms and mercy I see in the prescription of modest dress for all believers who may choose to adopt it in their lives, and this is why I decided to start practicing it.

Inner Peace: Adhering to the guidelines of Islamic modest dress brings inner peace to the individual for several reasons. As discussed above, modesty and striving to mould oneself in the Islamic manner helps to discipline our ego, which is the main source of personal ills. When I use the term "Islamic," I am particularly referring to the literal meaning of the word Islam, "submission." So a Muslim is someone who tries to submit her freewill to the truth. The truth is that we (and everything else around us) are being sustained and created continuously by God, and do not exist independently. Our ego, which is only one of the many faculties we have, is given to us as a tool. By striving to discipline its excessive desires, and channeling them to positive direction, we transform ourselves for the better. For instance, the ego falsely claims or wants to be independent. It does not like to recognize authority or feel gratitude. Hence, the challenge is to use the other faculties God has given us (such as our intellect and heart) to discipline our ego and submit our freewill to God's will. In Islam, human beings are not deemed to be intrinsically evil. We have the potential to rise higher than angels or fall lower than the level of animals. We have been given many faculties as tools to find and stay on the straight path. Submitting to the wisdom and compassion of God and obeying His recommendations about how we should dress is only one of many aspects of trust in God. Adhering to modest dress always reminds us that God is Ever-Seeing and that we are constantly in the presence of God. This is the utmost source of inner peace. Additionally, many women mention that wearing modest dress frees them from the pressures of society to be thin and to conform to fashion. Knowing that they are not being judged as feminine 'objects' helps enhance their self-esteem. When we dress and act modestly, others value us as human beings based on character and virtue.

Solidarity and Peace in Family Life: Family is considered a sacred unit in Islam. A peaceful marriage is essential for many reasons, one of which is the adequate upbringing of children. Breaking apart of families leads to many crisis for the family members as well as the society as a whole. That is why divorce is stated as the most unfavorable among the permissible practices in Islam. From the perspective of modest dress, there are two aspects of this practice that may help keep the solidarity of the family. If the husband is surrounded by women who have not adopted the pious manners and modest dress, he has a higher chance of cheating on his wife or worse, leaving his wife for another woman. Indeed, divorce caused by such reasons frequently occurs. The other aspect is, if the wife is flirtatious with other men and gives them leeway via her manners and dress, either due to jealousy or an actual affair, the family would again come under crisis. Human beings are innately jealous creatures. If their partner is engaging in an unlawful affair, both the man and the woman would be jealous, feel betrayed and their dignity will be in jeopardy. Statistics leave no doubt that these incidents are very common in both Western and Eastern societies in this century due to the decay of the role and importance of religion against the rise of materialism.

Thus, the Qur'an and the Prophetic traditions (*hadith*) on the matter of modest dress and manners aim to reduce these indecencies and preserve peaceful marriages as good role models for the children. Even though many examples of men and women who claim to be pious, yet engage in unlawful acts with the opposite sex may be cited, the ideal of Islam still proves to be true. God knows that human beings are imperfect creatures and the guidelines are there to set the perfect examples one should struggle to achieve.

Social Harmony: Islam does not only seek to guide the individual out of context of her surroundings. The realities of everyday life require human beings to interact with others unceasingly; hence social matters are also addressed in the Qur'an. Modesty of an individual's dress and manners automatically reflect on the society at large. Indeed, the problems of sexual-harassment of women and/or rape are wide spread in our societies. And only trying to catch and punish these people after the harm is done does not solve the problem. Individuals should reform themselves, learn good morals and values. Only in such a way can an entire society be reformed. When and if women practice ranges of nudity, the society at large is affected negatively. For instance, harmony among married couples and piety of individuals may deteriorate. This does not mean that only women must watch the way they act and dress, but as the Qur'anic verse 24:30 states, men are obligated to lower their gaze and adopt modest dress and manners as well.

Men are first warned to control themselves, and then, the required dress for men and women are complimentary for the decency of society. Also, reducing the debate only to the physical dress is indeed wrong and misrepresentative of Islam. God is concerned with our inner selves primarily. Thus, the modest dress serves its purpose only when it is appropriately complemented with the right morals and a whole Islamic way of life.

References

Al-Majlisi, M. *Bihar al-Anwar*. Beirut: al-Wafa, 1983.

Bayrak, Shaykh Tosun. *The Name and The Named*. Fons Vitae, 2000.

Esposito, John. *The Oxford Encyclopedia of Modern Islamic World*. Oxford University Press, 1995, (p. 108).

Lings, Martin. *Symbol and Archetype: A Study of the Meaning of Existence*. Malta, Quinta Essentia, 1991.

Mermer, Ali. "Divine Speech: The Ways to the Knowledge of God in the Risale-i Nur," in The Reconstruction of Islamic Thought in the Twentieth Century and Bediüzzaman Said Nursi, 24th-26th September, 1995. The İstanbul Foundation for Science and Culture. İstanbul: Sözler Publications, 1997.

Mermer, Yamine B. "Cause and Effect in the Risale-i Nur," in *The Reconstruction of Islamic Thought in the Twentieth Century and Bediüzzaman Said Nursi*, 24th-26th September, 1995. The İstanbul Foundation for Science and Culture. İstanbul: Sözler Publications, 1997.

_____. "Principles of Qur'anic Hermeneutics," *Journal of Scriptural Reasoning*, Vol. 5.1, (April 2005).

Muhammad, Sherif. "Women and their Legal Rights in Monotheistic Religions." *The Fountain*, Issue 41, Jan-Mar 2003, (p. 30-44).

Nasr, Seyyed Hossein. *Ideals and Realities of Islam*, ABC International Group, Chicago, 2000.

Nursi, Bediüzzaman Said. *Risale-i Nur Külliyatı*. Vol. 1-2. İstanbul: Nesil Yayınları, 2002 and 2004.

_____. *The Rays*, İstanbul: Sözler Publications, 1998.

_____. *The Words*, New Jersey: The Light, Inc., 2005.

Philips, Abu Ameenah Bilal. "Belief: The Purpose of Creation." www.viewislam. com/belief/purpose.

Turner, Colin. *Islam: The Basics*, Oxford: Routledge, 2005.